CARLO MARIA MARTINI

BIBLICAL MEDITATIONS

CARLO MARIA MARTINI

THE OUR FATHER

Do not heap up empty phrases

COVENTRY
PRESS

Published in Australia by
Coventry Press
www.coventrypress.com.au
33 Scoresby Road Bayswater VIC 3153
an imprint of Freedom Publishing Books
www.freedompublishingbooks.com.au

ISBN 9780648230380

English translation copyright © Coventry Press 2018

First published in Italy by Portalupi Editore 2005

Re-published by
© 2016 Edizioni San Paolo s.r.l,
Piazza Soncino 5 - 20092 Cinisello Balsamo (Milano) - ITALIA
www.edizionisanpaolo.it

Scripture quotations are from the New Revised Standard Version Bible: Anglicised Catholic Edition, copyright © 1989, 1993, 1995 the Division of Christian Education of the National Council of the Churches of Christ in the United States of America.

Catalogue-in-Publication entry is available from the National Library of Australia
http://catalogue.nla.gov.au

Printed in Australia by Brougham Press

An invitation 13

Introduction 17

THE FOUNDATION
(HOMILY)

The Eucharist at the Centre 25

1. MEDITATION
THE GOSPEL CONTEXT OF
THE OUR FATHER 29

The Our Father in Luke's Gospel 30

The Our Father in Matthew's Gospel 34

Some exegetical observations 36

Pointers for prayer 38

2. MEDITATION
"OUR FATHER WHO ART IN HEAVEN"   41
The Our Father and the Ignatian "Exercises"   42
The one whom Jesus calls Father   43
Pointers for prayer   51

SPIRIT AND WORD
(HOMILY)

Gentle, respectful belief   55
The power of the Word   58

1. MEDITATION
"HALLOWED BE THY NAME"   61
"Hallowed be thy name: – "holy" is your name   62
A beautiful, all-purpose set of meanings   64
Our attitudes   72

2. MEDITATION
"FORGIVE US OUR TRESPASSES
AS WE FORGIVE THOSE WHO
TRESPASS AGAINST US"   77
The context of the retreat   77
Asking for forgiveness   80
Freely offered forgiveness   82

Be perfect as the Father is perfect   84

Praying in truth   90

"I WAS SENT FOR THIS PURPOSE" (HOMILY)

It is God who waters and gives growth.   95

A free and courageous ministry   98

1. MEDITATION "LEAD US NOT INTO TEMPTATION"

     101

Sin, disorder, worldliness   102

Why speak of temptation?   103

Five types of temptation   105

Avoiding occasions of temptation   111

2. MEDITATION "BUT DELIVER US FROM EVIL"

     115

"Tear us away" from sinfulness   116

The wiles of the Evil one   122

Resisting the Evil one   126

UNLIMITED FAITH
IN THE WORD
(HOMILY)

A personal testimony   131

"All things are yours"   134

1. MEDITATION
    "THY KINGDOM COME"   137

    What is the Kingdom?   139

    Like yeast and seed   146

    The coming of the kingdom   147

    In hope and peace   148

2. MEDITATION
    "THY WILL BE DONE ON EARTH
    AS IT IS IN HEAVEN"   151

    Introductory Comment   153

    God's will in Jesus and in the disciples   157

    God's will in us   158

    So the heavenly Jerusalem will come   165

IN THE FREEDOM
OF THE SPIRIT
(HOMILY)

A model Pastor   169

The law of love   171

"It is the Lord who judges me"   173

1. MEDITATION
    "GIVE US TODAY
    OUR DAILY BREAD"   175

    What bread?   176

    Who is praying like this?   177

    Humility, filial trust, solidarity   181

CONCLUSION   185

AN INVITATION

The theme of this volume is the Our Father, which the Archbishop of Milan develops at a retreat he preached to priests. As is the case with the other books, the immediacy of the context and detailed references to circumstances experienced by the preacher and the retreatants make this text, which already appeared in print (Portalupi, 2005), a treasure trove of spontaneity and "everyday" worth.

The Cardinal Martini offers his listeners a series of reflections on the prayer taught by Jesus, seeing it, as did Tertullian, as the "summary of the whole gospel." Though it is true we are talking about a prayer everyone knows by heart it should not escape notice that the Our Father is "ever new, mysterious, versatile," indicative of a richness that only Christ could communicate, since we find there "a correspondence, a perfect correlation between the Our Father, the teaching of the gospel, the life of Jesus the Son of God, who died and rose for us."

This is true first of all for the "style" of the Our Father: following the example of Jesus himself, what distinguishes it is what it conceals, its economy of words and the perseverance and filial confidence with which it seeks not so

much the psychological gratification of "creating a beautiful prayer," but the abandonment to the Spirit who "intercedes for the saints according to the will of God" (Rom 8:27).

And that is the point. We are talking about *filial* confidence: the virtuous circle between fatherhood and sonship is what is called into play in the prayer Christ taught. With one strict condition: by teaching us to say "Father", Jesus did not simply point to a relationship of tenderness and affection with a God often surmised to be distant. He "involves us in his determination to fulfil the Father's will," so that "by saying this word we put our life and death on the line," making it the determining factor in the fundamental choices of our life, and we invoke its explosive force in the radical option that gives direction to our entire existence. (2nd meditation).

The invocation that opens the prayer, "hallowed be thy name," now acquires new light. It implies our involvement so that everyone will exalt the greatness of God and his works, without forgetting that the first and fundamental way of making God's name holy is through praise and gratitude.

Making his name holy is in fact "God's work first of all" and it is up to us in the first instance "to entrust concern for his glory to him." It is not up to us to "boost it." It is God himself who sees to it and we are asking that he manifests it. (3rd Meditation).

Enlightened by this glory, Christians seize upon the challenge of becoming active workers for reconciliation. Martini's words stress keenly the unprecedented nature

of the request for forgiveness in the Our Father: it is not enough to forgive the one who makes a mistake, but we need to take the first step so the other may have nothing against us. In an inversion of perspectives, to "forgive us our trespasses" is to enter into the Father's mercy, loving as Christ loved us. (4th Meditation). In a similarly disconcerting way, "lead us not into temptation" (5th Meditation), is also a commitment to avoiding occasions of temptation (Martini lists five types: seduction, contradiction, self-deceit, the silence of God and insignificance of Jesus). It is all one with the commitment to "resist the evil one" which opens up to the consolation of the Spirit and unmasks the wiles of the Adversary, his seductive, dispiriting, frightening, hidden cunning, his murky persuasion. (6th meditation).

The Cardinal offers a reflection on what, for many, is the central petition of the Our Father. The words "Thy kingdom come" mean Christians are not praying for a *de iure* restoration of a constituted order, but are committing themselves to energetically bringing it about. All the invocations, petitions previously commented on, contribute to it: hallowing God's name, forgiving trespasses, avoiding temptation, resisting evil. They all converge on the summons of the kingdom, something "not easily labelled, but it *is experienced in the following of Jesus day after day*, and by trusting the words of his gospel. It is something experienced by following Jesus, who at the outset of his public mission, humbly joined the queue of sinners at the Jordan, thus declaring that he wanted to proclaim the

kingdom in humility, hiddenness, by despising privilege."

This kingdom cannot be won; we can only ask that it come: "It is God who runs the kingdom, he who enters our hearts and wins them over; it is he, by the grace of the Holy Spirit, who takes possession of souls and transforms them into the image of Jesus. In other words, the *kingdom is Jesus*, his life, his way of living, loving, suffering." (7th Meditation).

Loving, believing, hoping like Christ, the human voice of the church prays that the kingdom will come in fulfilment of God's will (8th Meditation). By living like Christ, all human beings can make their "yes" a credible assent to the fire of love spreading across the world, generating children for the Father who is in heaven.

Giuseppe Mazza

INTRODUCTION

First of all, I would like to thank the Lord who once again allows me to offer a course of spiritual exercises, a retreat.

It is a great gift for me to meet each of you, to encounter your spiritual journeys and to walk with you a little way along them. Every time I preach a retreat, Paul's words at the beginning of the Letter to the Romans come to mind, where he says:

> For I am longing to see you so that I may share with you some spiritual gift to strengthen you – or rather *so that we may be mutually encouraged by each other's faith, both yours and mine* (Rom 1:11-12)

This common journey of faith also helps me.

It is useful to recall, at the beginning of a new experience, what a course of spiritual exercises is, because we often call Bible study weeks, catechetical update sessions, ascetic reflection, prayer meetings, "exercises".

These are wonderful, very useful things to do and they can also be used in a retreat or "the Exercises" properly so

called. But I think the central point is that these exercises, are a *Ministry of the Spirit* in which we listen to the Spirit so he can help us know God's will today, so we can embrace it and carry it out joyfully and confidently. The Spirit never leaves us static but has us dance, loosens us up , frees us of our stiffness.

So we need to create the best conditions in openness to the Spirit, for the Word to tell me and me alone what he wants of me now, this year, in my current state of health, with these relationships, these superiors, these difficulties and ill-feelings, these spiritual, social, political climates.

Hence we can also speak of a *ministry of immediacy*.

As Karl Rahner, the theologian, explains so well, God works in me immediately and speaks to my heart, seeks immediate contact with me and with each person's soul, to ask something he will not ask anyone else.

In the desire to help you enter these days with the right dispositions, I am suggesting you reply, maybe even in writing, to two questions.

The first: what are my feelings as I come to this retreat? Every year we come differently: on one occasion we were tired, out of sorts, disturbed, not feeling like it; another time we were ready and willing; on yet another we arrived full of distractions, bitterness, concerns, resentment; or we started the retreat wanting to focus on a particular issue burdening us. It is very useful to be aware of our state of mind.

The second question is: how would I like to leave this retreat? What grace would I particularly like to ask for so that I can leave content?

Over these days we could also edify one another by spending some time communicating in faith, during which those who wish to could simply express what has struck them most of all from everything they have heard, and which could also help someone else.

Each of you could also communicate with me personally in a conversation or put some thoughts in writing, a suggestion, a question, a reflection.

For my part the work is very simple: I will suggest some pages of God's word to you, some biblical thoughts, not for them to be the retreat theme (which is seeking obedience to the Holy Spirit) but as a background. And this time I have been inspired to choose the Our Father as the biblical background.

Someone could jump in and say: but we know it off by heart, we have said it an endless number of times. That is true, but it always has some surprises, is ever new, mysterious, versatile, and often we do not grasp all the wealth it contains. We can also consider the Our Father to be a summary of the Gospel.

It was no accident that Tertullian called it *breviarium totus Evangelii (a summary of the whole Gospel)*. That definition attracts me. My great and unforgettable spiritual father, Michel Ledrus, who died many years ago, used it as a title for one of his small booklets: (in English) *The Our Father, a Gospel Prayer*. It is a prayer which in fact sums up the whole Gospel; and, if we understand it well, we will see that only Jesus could say it and only he could teach it, because there is a correspondence, a perfect correlation

19

between the Our Father, the teaching of the gospel, the life of Jesus the Son of God, who died and rose for us.

I will briefly present some points for reflection on the Our Father, taking into account the exegesis found in specialised works. The collection of American commentaries on this prayer, entitled *Ermenèia*, dedicates a hundred very compact pages to the text, with dozens of pages of bibliography. We will not be doing an exegesis here, but we should bear in mind that there would be enough material on the Our Father to keep us busy for an entire year.

At this point the testimony left to us by the saints comes to mind. I am thinking, for example, of the vibrant exclamations St Teresa of Avila uses when she introduces her commentary on the opening words of the prayer in her *Way of Perfection*: "Our Father who art in heaven!'… "'Our intellect should be so captured and our will so penetrated that we no longer feel capable of saying these words…. How good it would be if here the soul could recollect itself, rise above itself to hear what this blessed Son is teaching it about the place where His Father lives when He says He is 'in heaven'!" (*Way of Perfection*, 27,1)

And again, it is beautiful to recall what St Theresa of the Child Jesus said when she recounted what Jesus' prayer suggested to her: "Sometimes, when my spirit is in such a dry state that it is impossible for me to pull out any thought to unite myself with the good God, I say an Our Father very slowly, and then the angel's greeting; then these prayers take over and nurture my soul much more than if I had said

them fast a hundred times." (*Manuscript* C 318). This was the Our Father for her.

One of her fellow Sisters attests: "Her union with God was continuous. She prayed without pause. One day I found her in her small cell. She was sewing quickly but she looked so recollected that I asked her why. 'I am saying the Pater' she told me. 'It is so beautiful to say the Our Father,' and tears welled up in her eyes."

This is our wish: to penetrate the heart, the spirit of the prayer Jesus taught us.

Lord Jesus, you see us here before you with a desire to pray more intensely over these days, but as is so often the case, we have come to you to ask: teach us to pray!

Our life experience shows us, year after year, that we do not know how to pray, that we constantly need to learn the right attitude for prayer. This is why we ask you to grant us your Spirit. We want you to teach us to pray like you taught St Ignatius Loyola, St Peter, St Paul, St Teresa of Avilia, St Therese Lisieux, all the saints. We would like to live the Our Father as you lived it. Grant that we may feel your support, your comfort, and that with our grace we can persevere in prayer over these days.

Mary, Mother of devotion, Queen of prayer, Patroness of our interior life, pray for us.

THE FOUNDATION
(HOMILY)

The Eucharist at the Centre

Each day the Eucharist will be the centre of all our work because it is the Lord Jesus who builds us up and meets us in the breaking of the bread. It is the Spirit who immediately touches us to change our heart, to get us to know God's will, to enrich us with the gift of discernment.

> You are God's building. According to the grace of God given to me, like a skilled master builder I laid a foundation, and someone else is building on it. Each builder must choose with care how to build on it. For no one can lay any foundation other than the one that has been laid: that foundation is Jesus Christ... Do you not know that you are God's temple and that God's Spirit dwells in you? If anyone destroys God's temple, God will destroy that person. For God's temple is holy and you are that temple (*1 Cor* 3:9-11, 16-17)

Now when Jesus came into the district of Caesarea Philippi, he asked his disciples, "Who do people say that the Son of Man is?" And they said, "Some say John the Baptist, but others Elijah and still others Jeremiah or one of the prophets," He said to them, "But who do you say I am?" Simon Peter answered, "You are the Messiah, the Son of the living God." And Jesus answered him, "Blessed are you, Simon son of Jonah! For flesh and blood has not revealed this to you, but my Father in heaven. And I tell you, you are Peter, and on this rock I will build my Church, and the gates of Hades will not prevail against it. I will give you the keys of the kingdom of heaven and whatever you find on earth will be found in heaven and whatever you loose on earth will be loosed in heaven (Mt 16:13-19).

In the readings of the liturgy today we find a significant word – one we will look at in the coming days – for St Ignatius of Loyola's *Spiritual Exercises*: the word is *foundation*. "No one can lay any foundation other than the one that has been laid; that foundation is Jesus Christ." And again in the Gospel: "You are Peter and on this rock I will build my Church."

So Christian life has a foundation: objectively it is Jesus, while subjectively it is faith in him. Everything we will say or experience over these days will come from this foundation which, in turn, is part of an even greater one: the

Mystery of God the Creator, Lord, friend of mankind. From such fundamental truths come all the rest.

The foundation which is God, Trinity, Love, the most perfect, merciful Being revealed in Jesus is then expressed in us through our obedience, acceptance of the Mystery and our quest for what it requires of us. Here is a summary of the retreat. It all starts with recognising God the Creator, Lord, Redeemer, who comes to us in Jesus and wants us to be with Him in the fullness of life. In our daily prayer and adoration we will return to Jesus and ask him to sustain us, nurture us and be our point of reference and support.

This foundation is then made concrete in time and space by Cathedral Churches – like the one we are celebrating in – which are the place where it is proclaimed and made visible.

Each of us can think back to his own Cathedral, diocese and local Church, through which he has been grafted onto Jesus Christ. It is only in this context that we find our truth and fullness. Thus we are invited in this celebration to pray for all the Churches in the world because it is in them that the mystery of God's love is revealed. Thinking of the Ambrosian Church I would like to recall that today it is celebrating 50 years since the death of Blessed Archbishop Alfredo Ildefonso Schuster, who was an important figure for the Church of Milan and for the whole Church of God.

Let us ask for the grace to always remain anchored in the local Church, in communion with the Pope, so that all our energy and action is not in vain but built on a rock, that everything we achieve over these days will be a consequence of our being Church.

Certainly during our retreat we should be concerned with ourselves, our ascetic life, God's will for us, but in the context and framework of the visible Church. In the *Exercises*, when St Ignatius talks about real choices, he says: "In the context of the visible Church." This is the opportunity for us to find our truth, the certainty that our journey is pleasing to God.

So let us pray that this journey is conducted in truth, objectivity, adherence to the Church, all it proclaims and constantly puts to us in its concern for us.

Let us renew our desire to serve this Church unselfishly, with dedication, fidelity, and loyalty. Only thus will we find Christ and enter that immediate relationship with God that he would like to establish with us over these days.

1

MEDITATION
THE GOSPEL CONTEXT OF
THE OUR FATHER

The first meditation I am offering you will be rather brief, and I would say a somewhat formal, exegetical introduction, though what we have said is still valid. I will divide it into three parts.

The first part is a *lectio* where we will spend time with the verses in *Lk* 11 and *Mt* 6 which refer to the Our Father. Then comes a *meditatio* in which I will offer some brief reflections on the contexts of the Our Father, the circumstances of its being taught. I will conclude with a *contemplatio* in which I would like to focus on the attitudes the various gospel passages suggest to us for these days.

We know that there are two Gospels which record the Our Father. This is astonishing because we would like there to be three; we would also like the Our Father to be in Mark. Exegetes discuss whether he did not refer to it because he did not know about it or because he was not concerned with passing on all of Jesus' words.

The Our Father in Luke's Gospel

Let us first of all read Lk 11. The context in which the Our Father is taught is Jesus' journey to Jerusalem which begins in 9:51, so already well into his life story. We recall that there is a tradition in Jerusalem which the basilica of the *Pater Noster* is testimony to, according to which the prayer would have been taught there, on the Mount of Olives, toward the end of Jesus's life. At any rate, for Luke the teaching of the Our Father came late in the piece.

- *"He was praying in a certain place"* (11:1a). This happened many times in Jesus' life: for example, the night before the selection of the twelve apostles (Cf. *Lk* 6:12); the night following the multiplication of the loaves, again near the lake ("He went up to the mountain by himself to pray " *Mt* 14:23); The morning of the beginning of his ministry at Carpharnum when he rose early and went to a place apart to pray ("In the morning, while it was still very dark, he got up and went out to a deserted place and there prayed" *Mk* 1:35); in Jerusalem, on Tabor, and yet again in other circumstances.

- It was on one of these occasions *"when he had finished"* (no one wanted to interrupt him seeing how recollected and focused he was)" one of his disciples said to him, *'Lord, teach us to pray.'"* (11:16). It is interesting that the question was put by one of the disciples, not by everyone, and not by a qualified disciple like Peter, James or John. He expresses the common desire the others did not dare put forward.

- And it goes on: *"as John taught his disciples"* (11:1c). We know nothing of the prayers the Baptist taught his disciples though it is probable that he gave them some pointers on

prayer as happened in the Qumran Community. But here we presume the Baptist taught his followers to pray.

It is not easy to understand what the disciple was really asking. We could turn to him and ask: explain to us what you wanted. Did you want Jesus to teach you the *content* you need for prayer? We could deduce this from the reply received, but still be surprised because the Jews already had plenty of content for prayer – it is sufficient just to think of the immense and rich content of the psalms. Or was your question about *how* to pray, the sort of thing Jesus points out in *Mt* 6:6: "Whenever you pray, go into your room and shut the door and pray to your Father who is in secret"? Or was it about the *external* manner: kneeling, eyes closed, in a place apart? Or was it about the *inner* disposition, the one *Luke* develops at length when he recommends perseverance in prayer (11:5-8) and says: "Ask, and it will be given you; search and you will find" (v.9)?

Which of the three hypotheses interprets the disciple's request? Probably all three. At any rate Jesus takes the question as a reference to content.

"He said to them, 'When you pray, say:
Father, hallowed be your name.
Your kingdom come.
Give us each day our daily bread.
And forgive us our sins,
For we ourselves forgive everyone indebted to us.
And do not bring us to the time of trial" (11:2-4).

The instruction is then prolonged in reference to the inner disposition, with which to pray. This is rather

extensive, while the prayer itself is very brief – three verses, five petitions elegantly put, precise.

Let us try to understand Jesus' words.

He begins with a concrete example:

> And he said to them, "Suppose one of you has a friend, and you go to him at midnight and say to him, 'Friend, lend me three loaves of bread; for a friend of mine has arrived and I have nothing to set before him.' And he answers from within, 'Do not bother me, the door has already been locked and my children are with me in bed. I cannot get up and give you anything.' I tell you, even though he will not get up and give him anything because he is his friend, at least because of his persistence he will get up and give him whatever he needs" (vv. 5-8).

It is a longer, more specific example of the Our Father. Jesus then moves on to a direct, threefold exhortation:

> So I say to you: Ask and it will be given you; search and you will find; knock and the door will be opened for you (vv. 9-10).

And again, a very clear example:

> Is there anyone among you who, if your child asks for a fish, will give a snake instead of a fish? Or, if the child asks for an egg, will give a scorpion? (vv. 11-12).

Then the conclusion:

> If you, then, who are evil, know how to give
> good gifts to your children, how much more
> will the heavenly Father give the Holy Spirit to
> those who ask him! (v.13).

It is interesting that none of the petitions of the
Our Father are picked up again here but it speaks of the
Holy Spirit. Perhaps this is why one of the very ancient
manuscript variants adds, after the request for daily bread:
"May your Holy Spirit come down on us and purify us."

Jesus begins from a real context from his own prayer,
and responds to a request first of all with content, then by
explaining at length the attitude of unflagging perseverance
in prayer. These attitudes of perseverance will be taken up
elsewhere in *Luke's* Gospel such as the parable of the unjust
Judge and the unfortunate widow:

> Then Jesus told them a parable about their
> need to pray always, and not to lose heart. He
> said, "in a certain city there was a judge who
> neither feared God nor had respect for people.
> In that city there was a widow who kept coming
> to him and saying, 'Grant me justice against
> my opponent.' For a while he refused; but later
> he said to himself, 'Though I have no fear of
> God and no respect for anyone, yet because
> this widow keeps bothering me, I will grant
> her justice, so that she may not wear me out by

continually coming.' And the judge said, 'Listen to what the unjust judge says. And will not God grant justice to his chosen ones who cry to him day and night? Will he delay long in keeping them? I tell you, he will quickly grant justice to them. And yet when the Son of Man comes, will he find faith on earth?" (18:1-8).

Such is the attitude Jesus stresses the importance of.

The Our Father in Matthew's Gospel

The Matthean context of the Our Father is situated within the Sermon on the Mount which includes Chapters 5-7 of the Gospel.

After the "but I say to you"s of Ch. 5, Jesus moves on in Ch. 6 to describe three acts of worship, of religion: almsgiving, prayer and fasting. He insists that none of them are to be done so that others can see them. It is in this context concerning the second act, worship, that the Our Father is inserted.

– In this case too, the description is quite extensive. Firstly Jesus stigmatises, so to speak, the prayer of religious hypocrites among the people: "And whenever you pray, do not be like hypocrites; for they love to stand and pray in the synagogues and at the street corners, so that they may be seen by others." Then comes the negative judgement: "Truly I tell you, they have received their reward" (6:5), that is to say, what they have done is of no value.

This is followed by accentuating the positive attitude: "But whenever you pray, go into your room and shut your door and *pray to your Father who is in secret*; and your Father who sees in secret will reward you" (v.6). It is an instruction firstly on the outward attitude followed by the inner one of prayer: in silence, recollection, in secret.

He then resumes the exhortation, referring to the Gentiles: "When you are praying, *'do not heap up empty phrases* as the Gentiles do; for they think that they will be heard because of their many words" (v.7). He is probably hinting at the endlessly recited monotonous invocation in the temples. I recall having seen in some plays or films and also when visiting Eastern monasteries or temples, the prayer wheel that is spun continuously so that the prayer is always repeated before God.

"Do not be like them, for your Father knows what you need before you ask him" (v.8). What is criticised is the prayer that pretends to tell God what we need. We note that there is a certain tension compared with the passage in Luke which says: be persistent in prayer. Jesus is warning: do not think that your insistence is magic.

– It is in this context that he teaches the Our Father:
"Pray then in this way:
Our Father in heaven,
Hallowed be your name.
Your kingdom come.
Your will be done,
on earth as it is in heaven.
Give us this day our daily bread.

———

And forgive us our debts,
as we also have forgiven our debtors.
And do not bring us to the time of trial,
but rescue us from the evil one (vv. 9-13).

It is a longer prayer than in Luke, which has two petitions plus a further three. In Matthew there are three, plus a further three and according to some, if we split the last one into two, we even have three plus four, that is seven petitions in all.

Jesus then adds something, by paraphrasing the penultimate petition:

> For if you forgive others their trespasses, your heavenly Father will also forgive you; but if you do not forgive others, neither will your Father forgive your trespasses (vv.14-15).

Some exegetical observations

Moving on to *meditatio* we can ask ourselves: Which of the two contexts is the most original? Which of the two formulas is the more ancient?

– Exegetes maintain (I think with good reason) that *the Lukan context is the more ancient*: We are not at the beginning of Jesus' public activity where he is speaking of plans for the future, but already somewhat into his ministry. And it is a concrete occasion when he was at prayer, a prayer immersed in lived experience. In *Matthew* by contrast, the teaching seems to be inserted into a sermon: "Do not heap up empty phrases.... Pray this way" (Cf. 6:7-9).

So we would say Luke's is the more likely context, though the issue does not affect the exegesis much.

There is also a question regarding the antiquity of the wording: Which is the older? Which is the shorter, the longer one?

There is agreement today on a kind of compromise: *Luke's wording is older* but *Matthew's is more original.* Matthew employs more archaic language, Luke has older content.

We will use both, but it still seemed useful to me to introduce you to the complex nature of the research.

– Exegetes also note that in *Luke* the prayer is the third of three pericopes coming one after the other: the parable of the Samaritan (Charity 10:29-37); the dialogue with Martha and Mary (Listen to the Word, 10:38-42); the Our Father prayer (11:1-4). It is as if to highlight the fact that charity, listening to the word, and prayer are inseparable.

– There is an interesting feature in Matthew's Our Father. Careful analysis shows that the Our Father is exactly at the centre of the Sermon on the Mount.

It is a teaching focus because we are warned that the Sermon on the Mount is only lived by someone who prays.

Pointers for prayer

In conclusion let me suggest some applications for personal prayer.

All of us, like the unnamed disciple, have said so often: "Lord, teach us to pray!" What were we asking for?

– I believe many people, when they put such a request, often want first of all to achieve inner unity, recollection, self-possession, the joy of composure characteristic of profound prayer. These are positive and useful attitudes but we are still within the ambit of *psychological prayer* aimed at obtaining certain benefits: learning to be calm, tranquil, recollected, reconciled, co-ordinated minus the uproar of thoughts racing through our head. People who take up Yoga or Zen learn similar things such as recollection, forgetting everything else, disengaging from the world outside, focusing on just one point or maybe on nothing, eliminating any thought in order to experience absolute calm.

Perhaps we also need such things to pray well. It takes a minimum of concentration and unity, just because prayer is also psychological health.

– Just the same, we want to ask Jesus to teach us to pray in the Spirit, especially to teach us inner disposition and what requests to put.

Often when I begin praying, I open the *Letter to the Romans* where it says that we do not even know how to pray as we ought (Cf.. 8:26) and I say: Lord, you can see that I do not know how to pray. But you have promised the Spirit to help me in my weakness, and the Spirit intercedes for me "with sighs too deep for words. And God, who searches

the heart, knows what is the mind of the Spirit, because the Spirit intercedes for the saints according to the will of God" (8:26-27).

So for me, for us, to learn to pray means learning to entrust ourselves to the Spirit who inspires us to say the Our Father, until we achieve that very beautiful state of mind I have meditated on so many times, in so many of life's circumstances: "When they hand you over do not worry about how you are to speak or what you are to say; for what you are to say will be given you at that time; for it is not you who speaks but the Spirit of your Father speaking through you" (Mt:19-20).

– Other than this fundamental disposition of abandonment to the Spirit as you make your way through the retreat I would like to suggest some others to you which Jesus has thrown light on.

We have seen four in particular: *hiddenness, simplicity and moderation of words, perseverance, filial confidence*.

In prayer before God each of you can choose which of these attitudes he needs most.

Filial confidence is certainly needed: the Father will never leave me without daily bread when I ask him for it.

Similarly needed is perseverance: over these days we will experience fatigue, heat, drowsiness, anxiety, dryness. Grant, Lord, that we may persevere!

And naturally we need hiddenness, because the retreat is hidden prayer *par excellence*, not known to the world, known only to God.

We also need a degree of simplicity and moderation which is not so much praying little but learning to pray in

a more relaxed way, generously, less anxiously; prayer that does not try to force God's hand, but where we entrust ourselves lovingly to him.

2

MEDITATION
"OUR FATHER WHO ART IN HEAVEN"

The booklet by Fr Ledrus I mentioned earlier begins thus:

> The Our Father represents the point of convergence of all the lines of gospel teaching. Every petition represents a world of considerations; behind each one we can marshal a number of Old and New Testament texts and discover the essential dimensions which articulate the entire evangelical message…. So in the Lord's Prayer we have a complete treatise of spiritual life arranged by the Lord himself: we will never adequately plumb it depths (*op. cit.,* p.8)

Personally, I feel quite unequal to the task of even attempting to determine some of the meanings of the prayer Jesus taught us. So I join with you in saying:

O God our Father, we know you only because your Son Jesus made known your name as Father. We do not know how to explain its profound meaning, but you give us the gift of experiencing it day after day. If you choose to, grant that

we may experience it with our mind and not simply with our heart, so we can enter into the thinking and heart of your Son Jesus Christ, who lives and reigns with you in the unity of the Holy Spirit for ever and ever.

The Our Father and the Ignatian "Exercises"

So, we place ourselves before the mystery of the Our Father. Naturally I do not intend to expound on it exegetically, as I have already said. What seems more important to me, rather, is to focus on some of the aspects of it in the spirit of St Ignatius' *Spiritual Exercises*, that is, bearing in mind the dynamic proper to those exercises.

It is a dynamic which develops by stages, over four weeks, and includes some powerful moments which help one understand what it means to follow Jesus in such a way as to make certain choices according to the Gospel.

It is in such a spirit that we would like to reflect on the Our Father, seeking the significance of certain words, individual petitions, and considering it within the framework of a journey seeking God's will.

The retreat, these "exercises" (as I reminded you) are a ministry of the Spirit, and they allow us to grasp what the Lord is asking, suggesting, commanding where each of us is concerned.

St Ignatius' booklet has an early page called *Principle and foundation*, which aims at establishing some co-ordinates by which to proceed in seeking God's will. For Ignatius,

Principle and foundation is the absolute sovereignty of God the Creator over everything, and human beings are bound to render him praise and service; and each one is called to choose that which best sets him (or her) on the path to serving God the Creator and Lord. This is a summation of the *Principle and foundation* which begins the *Exercises*.

We ask ourselves if the Our Father also has a *Principle and foundation*, and the reply is certainly in the affirmative. All the first part of the prayer constitutes the principle and foundation of everyday Christian life expressed in the last four petitions. However, I would like to dedicate myself this morning, in the spirit of the *Principle and foundation*, to reflecting on the first invocation, "Our Father who art in heaven." In the afternoon we will spend time with the words "hallowed be thy name," thus laying down the basis on which to pursue the journey over these days.

The one whom Jesus calls Father

The Our Father begins with the word "Father", which is not common. No psalm begins thus, and although in some prayers of the sacred texts we sometimes address God as Father, such a direct beginning is unique, even though Matthew expands on it more solemnly by comparison with Luke, "Our Father in heaven."

We will try to understand what the appellation "Father" is saying: what we mean by calling on him as "*our* Father" ; what we are adding by saying "Our Father [who art] *in heaven.*"

I suggest doing a *lectio* to respond to our questions, followed by a *meditatio* to understand the sentiments and directions for prayer it suggests for us.

• The word "Father"
– It is not in itself univocal ; it can have many meanings and arouse many emotions including existential ones, since each of us can relive his relationship with his own natural father. This might be excellent, fair, or poor. So it is an appellation that touches on many aspects of our interior life and psyche.

In general it is a word with many meanings. A father is first of all someone who gives biological life. Along with the mother he is its initator.

A father is also someone who educates to life, maybe quite strongly. The scriptures are not afraid to remind us that the father is also someone who disciplines. The *Letter to the Hebrews* reminds us that if we accept discipline from our earthly parent, we should not then be afraid if God the Father disciplines us, tests us, because the function of a determined educator is also typical of a father (Cf. 12:7-11).

A father is also someone who nurtures, who must procure sustenance for his children. He protects them and they can find shelter in his arms. A child throws himself into his father's arms looking for protection, closes his eyes while his father embraces him, in order not to see the danger. So the father is a symbol of refuge, comfort.

A father also represents the strength of tradition. When we call him that we immediately think of the roots that make up our identity as persons.

In the appeal to the "Father" which Jesus places on our lips, all these meanings are present.

– Just the same it is not enough, because if it were only this it would be an appeal, an invocation suited to everyone. Instead the mystery resides in the fact that while it is true that the Our Father can be said by anyone (I am thinking of the Jews and all who admit of a personal God), it is also true that the prayer Jesus taught us has very precise roots. Let me point to a particularly significant one: the baptism of Jesus.

He goes to the Jordan to be baptised by John. John tries to prevent him but Jesus insist, and John yields.

> And when Jesus had been baptised, just as he came up from the water, suddenly the heavens were open to him and he saw the Spirit of God descending like a dove and alighting on him. And a voice from heaven said, "This is my Son, the Beloved, with whom I am well pleased" (Mt 3:16-17).

Therefore, to say "Father" I need to have someone call me "Son". "Father" is not the first word but the second.

The first is the one of whom it is said: "Son, my dearest son, my beloved son".

So in the Our Father, Father is above all God the Father of Jesus Christ; it is He whom Jesus calls Father and by whom he is called Son, and he is strongly present throughout the Sermon on the Mount where Jesus nominates the Father eight times before we have the Our Father, and does so many times following it.

The Father is the Father of Jesus Christ and Jesus communicates his fatherliness, making us part of his own sonship.

St Paul states this clearly:

> For you did not receive a spirit of slavery to fall back into fear, but you have received a spirit of adoption. When we cry "Abba! Father!." (Rom 8:15-16).

Jesus gives us his Spirit and in his Spirit we can say "Father," Father of Jesus, my Father.

> ... It is that very Spirit bearing witness with our spirit that we are children of God and if children, then heirs, heirs of God and joint heirs with Christ – if, in fact, we suffer with him so that we may also be glorified with him (vv. 6-17).

If we consider that the generation of the Son by the Father is eternal, without time, that *today* God the Father is generating his Son, we understand *that at this moment* we are generated as sons.

Being sons of the Father is our identity; it is what defines us in the depths of our being. Its starting point is in baptism but endures throughout our life: the Father says to us: "My dearest son, my beloved son" and we respond with the word "Father".

Here is the first meaning of this word from which all the others derive: Father as nurturer, Father as educator, Father as refuge, Father as support, Father as comfort, also the

Father who disciplines and purifies because he has generated us in Christ.

Therefore we feel we are participating intimately in all of Jesus' prayer, which has the fundamental content of "Father, my Father." We perceive, if we visit Galilee and contemplate the mountains where he prayed, that our prayer is one with his. I made my own retreat on the Our father in June, on Mount Tabor, and I thought: I am joining Jesus who prayed at length while contemplating the Father.

We are one with him even in dramatic moments: "My Father, if it is possible let this cup pass from me!" (*Mt* 26:39); "Again he went away for the second time and prayed, 'My Father, if this cannot pass unless I drink it, your will be done.'" (v.44).

By teaching us to say "Father", Jesus involves us in his determination to carry out the will of the Father.

We are also encompassed within the attitude *Luke* describes at the conclusion of the passion: "Father, forgive them, for they do not know what they are doing" (23:24). To the extent that we succeed in forgiving, so do we share in Jesus' filial sentiments.

Above all, he involves us in the final words he spoke, according to *Luke's* description of the passion: "Then Jesus, crying with a loud voice, said, 'Father, *into your hands I commend my spirit.*'" (23:46). This is the journey he has us take by putting the word "Father" on our lips; a journey of love, trust, obedience, forgiveness, handing over our life. By saying this word we bring our life into play, and our death: "Father, into your hands I commend my spirit."

God's fatherhood, given to us in baptism, as I said, is both now and forever, and we bring it into being every time we pray, knowing that it has particular potency when we are taking important decisions. As St Thomas Aquinas says, at that moment the Lord gives us a supplement of the Holy Spirit hence a new proof of his fatherhood. We have to tackle so many decision-making situations in life: for example when someone takes on a new responsibility as parish priest, or becomes a bishop or the supervisor of a community; or when in secret we make a gesture of forgiveness, mercy, faith, hope. God's fatherhood is then expressed very strongly.

To conclude our reflection, it is beautiful to repeat the words of Peter and Paul who had intimately understood the mystery of Jesus' sonship and ours: "Blessed be the God and Father of our Lord Jesus Christ! By his great mercy he has given us a new birth into a living hope through the resurrection of Jesus Christ from the dead" (1Pt 1:31); and Paul at the beginning of his *Second Letter to the Corinthians*: "Blessed be the God and Father of our Lord Jesus Christ, the Father of mercies and the God of all consolation" (1:3).

• To the appellation "Father" Matthew adds "our" to emphasise that it is a collective, common prayer said together.

It is said in the first instance by the community of the sons and daughters of God, the baptised and, we can add, in the name of all the children of God, those whom Karl Rahner called "anonymous Christians" because by following their conscience, by the grace of love they are truly children

even though they do not know Jesus. Thus we say "Father" along with a multitude of people around the world.

And we say so especially with our community, with all those who live in daily fellowship with us. Again, by calling him "our" Father we are saying that God is the Father of all whom we have responsibility for.

Over the years of my episcopal service to the great diocese of Milan I have been much assisted by the certainty that God has been looking after each and every person entrusted to me who perhaps asked me for prayers and whom I cannot even remember. Today too every time I say "Our Father" I entrust to him all the people I have met and feel are unified with me in prayer, all who are nominally remembered before the Father.

He is, finally, the Father of all human beings because all are called to become Children of God. By saying "*Our Father*" we feel close to Buddhists, Moslems, non-believers whatever their life circumstances.

This way our prayer is broadened and embraces everyone.

Let us spend some time now on the "*Who art in heaven*". This expression can have many meanings.

The heaven-earth connection is called upon in the Gospels more often than we think:

"Truly I tell you, whatever you find on earth will be found in heaven" (*Mt* 18:18); "if two of you agree on earth about anything you ask, it will be done for you by my Father in heaven" (v. 19); "... so that your alms may be done in secret, and your Father who sees in secret will reward you" (Cf.. 6:4, 6:18. The "in secret" is "in heaven" in some translations).

If we seek something similar in the First Testament we can read, for example, in the First book of Macabees: "But as his will in heaven may be, so shall he do" (3:60)

"Who art in heaven." Then, is not in simple apposition. It certainly serves to distinguish the Heavenly Father from the earthly one, but with these words we are especially calling on the Father who lives in the world of transcendence, the ultimate world, the world of things that will never pass: the Father who lives in everlasting light where there is no ambiguity, no more insecurity, no more sin.

Heaven is also a place of reward where God's will is fully accomplished, perfectly.

This aspect of prayer has always filled me with great peace. In fact we are never in a clear, unambiguous situation, are always not quite there, on the cusp, and sometimes involved in compromise. Ours is an obscure, baneful situation where we can never really know if we are acting according to the Gospel or not; every day we are at risk of ambiguity by saying "Our Father who art in heaven": We are confessing that there is a place where everything is clear and unambiguous, resplendent, transparent, where everything is right and true. If we look around we are all wearied, burdened and sometimes oppressed by the mass of injustice surrounding us and which we are willy-nilly party to. By proclaiming "Our Father who art in heaven" we are affirming the existence of a situation where there is no more injustice, are no more tears, bitter moments, misunderstandings and everything is clarity, beauty, purity.

The initial invocation of the Our Father, then, can nurture, sustain and comfort our soul.

50

Pointers for prayer

What directions for prayer are suggested by the first invocation?

Some I have already indicated and I will sum them up by referring to the Gospels, especially the Sermon on the Mount.

– For example, one track we can follow as suggested to us is *abandonment, trust*: "But whenever you pray, go into your room and shut the door and pray to your Father who is in secret; and your Father who sees in secret will reward you" (*Mt* 6:6).

This is the Father from whom nothing escapes: not our sacrifices, our generosity, our secret humiliations, the silence we sometimes need to keep, to our disadvantage, in order not to involve others. This is the Father who pays back everything and to whom we abandon ourselves trustfully and totally.

This is the Father who takes care of us according to Peter's teaching: "Humble yourselves therefore under the mighty hand of God so that he may exalt you in due time. Cast all your anxiety on him, because he cares for you" (1 *Pt* 5:6-7).

The Father knows our needs before we pray to him.

Some days ago I found myself with some twenty or so Sisters whom I had guided 30 years ago on their way to final vows. We came together again to look back over the time passed. Personally, I used a very simple formula: over these 30 years God has taken care of me much more than I could have foreseen or asked for or demanded; so he will continue to look after me.

———

This track is abandonment, absence of any concerns: "Cast all your anxiety on him because he cares for you."

Then there is the track of *entrusting all the people we love and all the situations that oppress us, to him.* While living in the Middle East, in Jerusalem, I witnessed situations of violence and oppression daily, and one truly does not know how to escape the confusion. One feels blocked, involved, constrained, confused.

Yet the invocation "Our Father who art in heaven" invites us to say: Lord you know the meaning of everything that is happening and you will confirm those who are right and will give justice to those who ask for justice.

Let us question ourselves seriously, then, on our ability to at least partly carry out the suggestions that come from the word "Father"; let us question ourselves on whether it is anxiety or peace that prevails in us. We certainly have many reasons for being anxious. But if anxiety prevails in us as a basic sentiment it means we cannot truthfully say the word "Father".

If we say it seriously, then the prevailing sentiment in us is one of deep peace.

Likewise, let us ask ourselves if sadness or joy prevails in us. If sadness, bitterness, pessimism, scepticism prevail, perhaps scepticism about the Church, society, it means we do not seriously entrust ourselves to God the *Father,* because it is He who cares for everything, He who knows and puts everything in order, He who knows how to bring it all home.

Hence trust, joy, abandonment are sentiments that put us on the Gospel path. It is not by chance that the Our Father has been described as "a summary of the Gospel"

SPIRIT AND WORD
(HOMILY)

The texts from today's liturgy touch on two themes we have already said to be central to our retreat: the Spirit and the Word.

Gentle, respectful belief

The spirit searches everything, even the depths of God. For what human being knows what is truly human except the human Spirit that is within? So also no one comprehends what is truly God's except the Spirit of God. Now we have received not the spirit of the world, but the spirit that is from God, so that we may understand the gifts bestowed on us by God. And we speak of these things in words not taught by human wisdom but taught by the Spirit interpreting spiritual things to those who are spiritual.

Those who are unspiritual do not receive the gifts of God's Spirit for they are foolishness to

them and they are unable to understand them because they are spiritually discerned. Those who are spiritual discern all things, and they are themselves subject to no one else's scrutiny.

"For who has known the mind of the Lord so as to instruct him?"

But we have the mind of Christ (1 Cor 2:10-16).

We recall first of all that we described the retreat as a ministry of the Spirit and of immediacy because according to the words of St Paul read to us today, the Spirit scrutinises the depths of God and of our own heart. It is He who makes possible the immediate contact of the inexpressible, ineffable, beyond the human Mystery with our own little story.

The Apostle goes on to say: "We have received ... The Spirit that is from God, so that we may understand the gifts bestowed on us by God." He has given us his fatherhood and with this our Christian vocation, then our priestly and religious vocation, the vocation to various kinds of service, and also the vocation to the cross and suffering. The Spirit speaks to us of all this.

Paul's letter teaches us that "those who are spiritual discern all things," given that they have the perception, wisdom, sensitivity that allows them to understand and savour things in a profound way. By contract the unspiritual do not understand "the gifts of God's Spirit"; if they try to do so they notice that these things are above and beyond

their experience and end up saying: this stuff belongs to another world.

It can happen to us that there comes a time when we have moved away from a prayerful, faithful milieu, an atmosphere of openness to heavenly things, and we no longer understand the voice of the Spirit. It is then that we fall into serious temptation against faith: almost as if we seem to be reasoning with unbelieving eyes, and the believer's situation seems crazy. Only the power of the Spirit – which comes from persevering prayer, faithful practice of the sacraments, self-control – resituates us in the truth of the life of faith.

It is risky to meddle with what Paul calls the "unspiritual" or "natural", psychic situation, because one loses the delicate, keen, tender, respectful sensitivity the Church Fathers used called the *pius credulitatis affectus*, that gentle, respectful belief which allows us to perceive "spiritual things" as real. Instead when we surround ourselves with a worldly, profane, secular atmosphere, everything looks hazy and grey to us. Unfortunately we are particularly subject to such temptation, because we are on the frontier between two worlds: we live in the world of the things of God but at the same time find ourselves in contact with the world of everyday profane things. If we have not clearly decided on our position we shunt between both situations and our judgement is unsure, obfuscated, often muted, bland.

The temptation to atheism and non-belief is always at the door. We know that St Theresa of the Child Jesus lived the

final years of her life amid a terrible trial of unbelief, seeing and judging things as the non-believer does. Despite it all she had the grace of persevering in faith.

In the final months of her life she also wrote very beautiful, simple poems full of faith. To anyone who asked her how she could do so amid so many temptations and so much darkness while heaven seemed so agonisingly closed to her, she replied: "*I sing what I want to believe.*" Faith had become willpower in her, sustained by the Spirit.

The retreat is an opening, an exercise in making room for the Spirit. It allows us to accept him as a child accepts the kingdom, it allows us to admit him, accept and follow him, to gradually rediscover that overview of things with which we can breathe peacefully. Then we will no longer be half atheist, half believers, but heart felt believers.

The power of the Word

He went down to Capernaum, a city in Galilee, and was teaching them on the Sabbath. They were astonished at his teaching, because he spoke with authority. In the synagogue there was a man who had the spirit of an unclean demon, and he cried out with a loud voice, "Let us alone! What have you to do with us, Jesus of Nazareth? Have you come to destroy us? I know who you are, the Holy one of God." But Jesus rebuked him, saying "Be silent, and come out of him!" When the demon had thrown him down

before them he came out of him without having done him any harm. They were all amazed and kept saying to one another, "What kind of utterance is this? For with authority and power he commands the unclean spirits, and out they come!" And a report about him began to reach every place in the region (Lk 4:31-37).

The retreat (as we are reminded by the second reading) is also an opening to the Word, the strong and effective Word. The Word of Jesus is not simply interpretation of, commentary on sacred texts, like rabbinical teaching could be. He speaks in God's name.

We are still under the influence of the Word today. It is the Word of baptism which makes us sons and daughters; it is the Eucharistic word that has us take important decisions involving our entire existence, an existence which is permanently bound up with Jesus' fidelity.

It is the Word which casts the world and the demon from us. It is not necessarily an unclean demon; it can be, but in general the Word is strong when we become bewildered, mentally agitated and confused. Then the Word re-animates us, recreates us, regenerates us, as Peter says: You have been born anew through the living word of God (Cf. 1 Pt 1:23).

How often we, I, have experienced the Word giving me back courage, relaunching me, clarifying things, re-ordering my thinking, offering me a newly opened horizon!

The retreat is about letting the Word resound in us with the power of the spirit.

In this Eucharist we ask that we may be open to the grace of the spirit and the Word, a Word which, as we always need to remind ourselves, is revealed in its truth when we begin to put it into practice.

And we begin to grasp something of the very Mystery of God when we see that it is energy, action, gift, renunciation, service, and when we agree to enter into this dynamic and be in harmony with God's life which is dedication without limits. Then the Mystery comes back to us clearly, otherwise it remains a concept which drowns in the sea of philosophical objections.

The Eucharist is a gift without limits, given us to know and accept.

1

MEDITATION
"HALLOWED BE THY NAME"

Let us return briefly to the theme from this morning's meditation to introduce us to reflection on the invocation that follows: "Hallowed be thy name."

Fr Michel Ledrus explores several words which appear to me to really express what we tried to explain when commenting on the word "Father":

> First of all, the term "Father" was a title of honour for the divinity among Greeks and Romans, rather than a reminder of fatherly tenderness. Instead when the Christian calls God his "Father" he is testifying to the remission of sins, righteousness and holiness regained as a result of the redemption; filial adoption, being eternal heirs, and the freely given guidance of the Spirit. (*op. cit.*, pp. 18-19)

This is the Christian meaning of the invocation when said in the Spirit of Jesus Christ. He goes on to say:

> The exclamation "Father", then, expresses the mysterious, intimate knowledge of God

possessed by the faithful individual who says the Our Father under the action of the Holy Spirit (*ibid* p. 20).

Monstra te esse Patrum: show you are a Father! "Show us your steadfast love, O Lord."

(Ps 85:7). All praise of God is focused on the word "Father". Christ's work is taken up in manifesting God's fatherhood: "I have made your name known to those whom you have me from the world: (Jn 17:6) (*ibid* pp. 21-22)

These words help us to consider the following expression of the Our Father, "Hallowed be thy name," which we will continue to meditate on in the spirit of the *Principle and foundation*, the principle on which the entire dynamic of the Ignatian *Exercises* and the entire dynamic of Christian life are based.

"Hallowed be thy name: – "holy" is your name

The wording is uncommon, a little strange, words we do not use when preaching and perhaps not even in prayer outside the Our Father. We would probably have preferred the Greed verb *agiasthéto*, "be made holy," or another verb we feel more at ease with, the verb *doxàzo* (glorify).

Doxàzo appears extensively in Jesus' final prayer, as found in John's Gospel, and we understand its meaning very well: "Father, the hour has come, glorify your son so that the son may glorify you" (17:1), "I glorified you on earth

by finishing the work you gave me to do" (v.4); "So now, Father, glorify me in your own presence with the glory that I had in your presence before the world existed" (v.5); "All mine are yours and yours are mine; and I have been glorified in them" (v.10); " The glory that you have given me I have given them so that they may be one as we are one" (v.22); "Father, I desire that those also, whom you have given me, may be with me where I am to see my glory which you have given me because you loved me before the foundation of the world" (v. 24).

We would have found ourselves more comfortable language-wise if the Our Father had used the verb *doxàzo*: "Father, glorify your name" or "your name be glorified."

The verb *agiàzo* (*agiasthéto*) is certainly more mysterious, a little less elegant, more difficult to penetrate the meaning of.

Nevertheless it is important for us to understand the meaning of this invocation so I would like us to pray to the Father saying: your name is great, your name is glorious. Grant that we may probe the intention of your son when he placed the words "Hallowed be thy name" on our lips.

Let us ask the Virgin Mary, who had a profound perception of the mystery of the holiness of God's name, to illuminate our mind and heart so we may grasp the attitudes these words wish to stir up in us, and glimpse the Christian journey they invite us to take.

In recalling the figure of Mary, her song, the *Magnificat*, comes to mind where she sings joyfully: "for the Mighty One has done great things for me / and holy is his name" (*Lk* 1:49).

—————

63

Perception of the holiness of the Name is typical of the Old Testament. Further on I will quote some passages from the Prophets. We are asked to enter into the mentality of the First Testament, since the invocation "Hallowed be thy name" is on the border between the First and Second Testaments. They are words the Jews almost understand better than Christians, and Jesus places them in our heart and on our lips because he wants to anchor ourselves in the First Testament.

So I propose to do a *lectio* where we ask ourselves what this "Name" means and what "*hallowed be* thy name" means. I will then offer you some points for a brief *meditatio*, an application: what attitudes does such a prayer suggest to us?

A beautiful, all-purpose set of meanings

1) We ought not be surprised if we do not find precise answers to our questions, because the Our Father is a rich, intense, very short prayer packed with many meanings. Obviously of its nature, prayer is not a mathematical formula, so it is possible to find many meanings, and they are probably all valid.

We see this already by considering the word "name". We know from the First testament that "Your Name" means "your person", "your power", "your being", "your reality".

But just the same we ask: does it mean that God is to be acknowledged as God and from that comes the command in Mt 22:21: "Give.... to God the things that are God's"? Or is it "Hallowed by your *name* as *Father*", that is, that everyone

acknowledge you not just as God but as the Father, the tender, loving, merciful Father who sends his Son for the forgiveness of sins? Or that everyone acknowledge your greatness, power, infinity, transcendence? Or that everyone recognise in particular your kindness, your interest in human beings and readiness to indulge them? It probably means all of these. Personally I would opt for insistence on: hallowed be your name *as Father*; that is, that you be acknowledged as the One who loves, comforts, forgives, as the One who in the words of the parable of the prodigal son, awaits, goes out to embrace, puts on the wedding garment, prepares a great feast (Cf. *Lk* 15:11-32). The prayer does not say so. It is up to us to explore one or other aspect.

2) What does "hallowed" mean? I have already said it is a curious, strange expression.

• It could be a simple *doxology* ("Father, blessed be your name, your kingdom come"), a kind of apposition, an insertion of the kind often found in Jewish prayers.

Yet I do not think this hypothesis is probable.

We could also refer to the *berakha*, a common Hebrew literary genre. In fact when a guest is met or invited, they say: *baruk ha bà*, blessed is the one who comes; and to the question, How are you? They reply: well, thank you, *baruk ha shem,* blessed be your Name.

The use of the *berakha*, blessing God, has its application in so many other aspects of life: there is the *berakha* before eating, the one Jesus said over the bread and wine, the prayer of blessing; there is the *berakha* after meals, and so on.

The concept can also be seen in the New Testament. Elizabeth's greeting to Mary, for examples is a *berakha*:

"*Eulogeméne sy en gynaixin*", "Blessed be the fruit of your womb, Jesus (*Lk* 1:42). It is here that we see the verb *berek* with a corresponding verb *eulogein* (*eulogeméne*) and the term *eulogìa*.

The Benedictus begins with a *berakha*; "*Eulogetòs kyrios o theòs tou Israel*" (*Lk* 1:68). We find another form of *berakha* in *Lk* 11:27: "a woman in the crowd raised her voice and said to him, '*Blessed is the womb that bore you and the breast that nursed you!*'".

And there are at least two New Testament letters which begin with a *berahka*. The *Second Letter to the Corinthians*: "Blessed be the God and Father of our Lord Jesus Christ, the Father of mercies and the God of all consolation" (v.3); the *Letter to the Ephesians*: "Blessed be the God and Father of our Lord Jesus Christ, who has blessed us in Christ with every spiritual blessing in the heavenly places" (v. 3).

At any rate, the literary genre of the *berakha* does not seem to me to fully correspond to the invocation of the Our Father, "Hallowed be thy name."

• Instead it is more probably a true and proper *petition*, a *request*.

What is it asking? Different things can be considered.

In the spirit of the Prophet Ezekiel who uses wording of this kind more often, the request could mean: "*Father, act, intervene in our history* so your name may be recognised as great." The prophet asks for God's intervention to amaze the people, who will then exclaim: God is truly great!

"I will sanctify my great name," that is, I will manifest myself with works that will astonish, make my name

praised, "Which has been profaned among the nations and which you have profaned among them." You, by your behaviour, have acted in such a way that the people despise my name; now I will show its greatness. "And the nations shall know that I am the LORD, says the LORD God, when through you I display my holiness before their eyes" (Cf. Ez 36:21 ff.).

"Hallowed be thy name" is a theological passive, that is: *You* sanctify your name, intervene in this dark, confused, violent, evil world; intervene to show you are here, that you are just, holy, have the destiny of history in your hands.

Ezekiel even emphasised a series of seven sanctifying interventions of God's:

> I will take you from the nations, and gather you from all the countries, and bring you into your own land. I will sprinkle clean water upon you and you shall be clean from all your uncleannesses, and from all your idols I will cleanse you. A new heart I will give you, and a new spirit I will put within you; and I will remove from your body the heart of stone and give you a heart of flesh. I will put my spirit within you, and make you follow my statutes and be careful to observe my ordinances. Then you shall live in the land that I gave to your ancestors (vv. 24-28a).

These are all interventions to reconstitute lost Israel and which therefore glorify God: seven interventions concluding with the formula of the Covenant: "You shall be

my people and I will be your God" (v. 28b). Still today the Jewish people live in this hope and the presence in Israel of millions of Jews gathered from all peoples is seen as a glorious intervention of God who always loves his people.

It is also interesting to read Is 29:22-23:

> Therefore thus says the LORD, who redeemed Abraham, concerning the house of Jacob:

> No longer shall Jacob be ashamed, No longer shall his face grow pale, For when he sees his children, the work of my hands, in his midst, they will sanctify my name; they will sanctify the Holy One of Jacob, and will stand in awe of the God of Israel.

Therefore I believe that we see in the expression "hallowed be thy name" a vocabulary of sanctification, of holiness, of *kadosh*, of the Holy One. It seems to me that it can best be translated with the word *transcendent*: that God's transcendence be acknowledged, that God be recognised as transcendent and that he carry out works in history which make everyone cry out: God is great!

At this point I turn once more to the study by Fr Ledrus. He contradicts the view that many, including Schürman, have that the Our Father contains just one invocation – "thy kingdom come" – around which all the others are situated. In a certain sense that is true. But the very request "thy kingdom come" is subordinate to the one before it: that God's name be glorified and blessed, that He be acknowledged in his transcendence, his holiness, as Father so, reading from his text:

———

"Father, hallowed be thy name" (Lk 11:2). This version of St Luke's shows how the first aspiration ("hallowed be thy name") is tied to invocation of the Father, while at the same time detached from the aspiration which follows and all the petitions that follow but which will be referred to this same exaltation of God (*op. cit.,* p. 33).

So, in the first place "hallowed be thy name" and therefore "thy kingdom come," "thy will be done," fulfil certain necessary conditions such as daily bread, forgiveness, freedom from temptation and evil.

This expression lifts the prayer up to the level of a Eucharistic hymn charged with jubilee tones. Thus it also flourishes on the lips of Christ who, with eyes raised to heaven, prayed, "Holy Father" (Jn 17:11); "your name" means your Person; not just as the determination but also the manifestation of power, omnipotent mercy (Cf. Is 59:19): "name-glory"; Zech 14:9: "the Lord will be one and his name one." It means God as he is revealed and as he shows himself in his plan of salvation, and hence just as he is known by us in faith through the communication of the presently dim understanding God has given of himself.

Hallowed means: "May God be exalted, acknowledged as incomparable" [transcendent]; may God be glorified in carrying out his plan

of love: "I made your name known to them and I will make it known, so that the love with which you have loved me may be in them, and I in them" (Jn 17:6). Christ's highest concern, the sole passion of his heart, was God, God alone; this he passed on to his disciples also in the prayer he taught them; thus before dying he could say: "I have made your name known to those whom you gave me" (Jn 17:6).

Jesus came to teach us to "sanctify God's name," that is, to treat God as God and not deal with anyone other than God and his glory, to love him with the greatest, most exclusive love and exalt him above all else, especially above ourselves, and never place him in our heart in competition with any earthy god; to be his enthusiasts. The security and trust that Jesus manages to communicate to us by teaching us to pray this way, makes us feel that this desire has already been heard, in the sense that God is already manifesting his mercy and glory in the world, and is already fulfilling his plan of salvation. In the final analysis God alone is the author of his own glorification, and whoever prays as Jesus has taught us knows how to share in it and desires it to be fulfilled in himself and everyone today, and above all in the royal manifestation he will make of himself at the end of the world (Ez 36:23) (ibid pp. 33-34).

———

Finally, I remind you that something similar is also found in Jn 12:27-28 with the verb *doxàzo*, typical of the Evangelist as we have seen:

> "Now my soul is troubled. And what should I say – 'Father, save me from this hour?' No, it is for this reason that I have come to this hour. Father, glorify your name." Then a voice came from heaven, "I have glorified it, and I will glorify it again."

Intervene, O Father!

Here we are speaking of the glorification which is Jesus' death and resurrection. The Father is sanctified in the risen Christ. Perhaps when Jesus went to the Jordan to be baptised he was already praying for the sanctification of God his Father.

In any case, the appeal in the Our Father is stated in the passive and does not make this content explicit.

– Another nuance of meaning, then, is possible: the desire that *we be the ones who praise God's name.*

The invocation "hallowed be thy name" is understood by many Christians to be a resolve to give praise to God's name and not blaspheme. So "hallowed be thy name" or "may your name be made holy *by us* human beings."

It is the honour which is God's due, which the prophet *Malachi* speaks of: "A son honours his father, and servants their master. If then I am a father, where is the honour due me? And if I am a master, where is the respect due me? Says the LORD of hosts to you, O priests, who despise my name" (1:6), priests who were not acting according to the laws of Moses and so were not honouring God.

Considered at greater depth, by entering into communion with Jesus, human beings can sanctify themselves, hence they are hallowing God's name by their lives. A significant passage of John's Gospel suggests this, where the same verb *agiàzo* of the Our Father occurs; "Sanctify them (*agziàson*) in the truth.... And for their sakes I sanctify (*agiàzo*) myself, so that they may be sanctified (*òsin egiàsmenoi*) in truth" (17:17-19), thus giving testimony to God's holiness.

The very simple supplication "hallowed be thy name" remains, as you can see, a little mysterious, holds different meanings, includes God's action and human action: *intervene, show yourself* and *grant that we may also praise you, glorify you, make holy your name.*

It is up to each of us, when we say the Our Father, to allow the Spirit to lead us, enjoying one or other of the contents of this supplication.

Our attitudes

I will now attempt to reply to the earlier question in our *meditatio* and *contemplatio*: Which attitudes does saying these words suggest, support, encourage? What does someone who prays this way have in his heart as he says these words?

– First of all I think the sense of *praise* and gratitude to God should come to us spontaneously. What comes to mind is the moment prior to the raising of Lazarus where *John* records: "And Jesus looked upward and said, 'Father, I thank you for having heard me. I know that you always hear me" (11:41).

Whoever prays this way should necessarily have this tone of constant gratitude in his heart, a tone St Paul made his own in his letters. For example we recall the beginning of the *Letter to the Colossians*: "In our prayers for you we always thank God, the Father of our Lord Jesus Christ" (1:3).

This verse strikes me because I have known few priests capable of thanking God for their community. By contrast I have known many who have complained: the people do not respond, do not listen, don't come. They had real reasons for their discomfort but I used to tell them: the fact that your community exists is already a miracle of God's; the fact that the baptismal faith in the Gospel is alive in a pagan and unbelieving world is a miracle of God's, so in the first instance thank God for this. It is the attitude the apostles had: give praise to God who called you to the Faith. We are sinners, very imperfect, extremely negligent, but we have an extraordinary gift which has spread among Christian people – faith and hope I would like every priest to be warmly grateful for to the Lord for himself and his faithful, praying thus: I give you thanks, Father, because you called those sons and daughters of yours from the darkness of ignorance to a knowledge of you who are Love.

Gratitude for everything the Lord does through love seems to one to be the underlying attitude to the invocation, "hallowed be thy name", which can flow from awareness of God's gifts and can abound in blessings, as the *Letter to the Ephesians* says: "... giving thanks to God the Father at all times and for everything in the name of our Lord Jesus Christ" (5:20).

Nurturing this attitude which makes us lift up our heart to God, is something very healthy and unfortunately little evident in our Christian Communities which usually, at least in the West, Complain and are too inwardly focused, always ready to see what is not working.

Whoever has read my retreat books from past years knows that I usually insist on this also in the penitential conversation. This should begin with giving thanks to God, praising the Lord for what he has done for me since my last confession. When I am hearing confessions and the people begin to run through their sins, I immediately interrupt and ask: but have you nothing to thank God for? And I hear the reply: yes, it is true. I do have some things. Suddenly the atmosphere changes, the inner disposition changes.

This attitude of praise is one we find only in Paul's later Letters but also in the very first, the *Letter to the Thessalonians*: "Rejoice always, pray without ceasing, give thanks in all circumstances; for this is the will of God in Christ Jesus for you" (5:16-18).

This is what the invocation in the Our Father is reminding us, it seems to me; when it invites us to praise God, give thanks, to want the Father blessed for his greatness, a greatness which will appear and be made manifest, clearly evident.

Let us ask ourselves: is thanksgiving the underlying tone of my life? When I wake in the morning is my first thought addressed to the Father: thank you, Lord, for you are so great and good, because you have loved me and preserved me this night? In the evening am I grateful for the gifts received?

– A second direction to explore:

From what we have said while trying to explain these words it seems that making his name holy is firstly God's work, it is He who glorifies his name. It follows that we are invited to *entrust concern for his glory to him.*

It is not up to us to "inflate it". It is God himself who sees to it and we are asking that he manifests it. Sometimes we behave as if his glory depends on us.

I remember a famous theologian from Milan, Bishop Pino Colombo, ironically saying that sometimes we seem to want to practise artificial respiration on Jesus Christ to make him rise! It is a serious mistake because he is life, resurrection, glory.

– A third very important attitude is that of someone who realistically believes God's glory has been much trampled on in the world, especially where human dignity has been trampled on, and this happens pretty much everywhere.

From this comes the *prayer of intercession* that ambiguous situations and God's apparent silence be surmounted. It is then that we can allow ourselves some complaint as we find in the psalms: Where are you Lord? Where is your glory? Why do you hide yourself? Why do you not reveal yourself? Why do you not show yourself?

Even so, this kind of questioning should be done within the framework of joy and confidence we described earlier. Many devout Jews, even in the darkest moments of their history, have known and still know today, how to pray thus: Lord, you are hiding yourself; you seem to be silent. Show your glory! Where are you, Lord? Grant that we may see

you. Grant that all may recognise that you are our king, that you are looking after us, that you have not abandoned us.

If we have properly accepted this profound sense of praise of God, we can then complain to Him, but in the spirit and attitude of faith and intercession.

2

MEDITATION
"FORGIVE US OUR TRESPASSES
AS WE FORGIVE THOSE WHO
TRESPASS AGAINST US"

News of the tragedies which made yesterday such a
sad day, the attacks in Israel, Moscow and Iraq, urge me
to present a consideration on the context we are living in
during these days of retreat.

The context of the retreat

Firstly there is the context of our lives, one I asked you
to reflect on with two questions: how am I as I come to the
retreat? How do I want to leave it?

As we know this context is situated within an ecclesial
framework: my diocese, my community, my local Church,
the universal Church. We should always keep these things
in mind in our prayers.

The third setting is the general socio-political one
characterised by three phenomena: powder-kegs of
co-existence, the prevalence of group interests, the
absurdity of evil.

Firstly the *powder-kegs of co-existence.* It is more essential today than ever for diversity and difference to be converted to co-existence. This means not living in ghettoes or destroying one another, but it is also more than just tolerating one another. There is still very little real tolerance. Co-existence seems to be a good solution but it is not enough. What is needed is co-existence where we are all leaven for one another and not necessarily in any proselytising sense where you will convert to my religion, my culture before we can create unity.

While an evangelising perspective remains fundamental for the Christian, we first have to realise the possibility of being together in our differences in such a way that my way of living gives me authenticity and helps the other to appreciate his or her life, and discover what the Lord is saying in the depths of their heart, be these religious or non-religious words.

Dialogue among religions is certainly useful but I do not see it as so important. By their nature religions are fixed and codified systems, and at best they can exchange courtesies, information, clarifications to avoid misunderstanding, but they remain much as they are. Furthermore we always see the same people at the numerous interreligious dialogue meetings, going from one continent to another talking peace and giving lectures here and there.

This is not enough. I repeat that we need to coexist by being leaven for one another, each living in his or her authenticity and acting in such a way that the other is encouraged along the way to even greater authenticity with regard to their own tradition and religion.

Seen this way, there is a need for us to have strong authenticity, not so much in terms of our socio-cultural, socio-religious identity as our evangelical identity, because in some ways the Gospel is supra-confessional. For example, the sermon on the Mount has no confessional label attached to it. It renews human existence as such and can be worth anyone's while to follow.

I conclude: the powder-keg coexistences we see around the world – from the Holy Land to Bosnia, Rwanda, Sudan – are a demonstration of the need for differences to be able to coexist; in the opposite case, humanity will not survive.

– The second phenomenon consists in the fact that *group interests* prevail in the socio-political context.

In our region and even more so in others, the sense of the common good is very weak. There is the good of the family, the clan, which in certain countries is like steel armour-plating and goes to the extent of murder when internal laws are not respected and the family is dishonoured. Even though it is true that clan spirit can have a positive side, it can also be a form of defence within an anarchic or authoritarian society.

Nonetheless we need to journey toward a world where the common good is the prime value; not only the good of the group, race, not even of the nation, but the good of humanity as a whole.

Christianity has much to say about breaking down a context of group interests, precisely because it proposes a common, concrete and universal good.

Finally, we must not forget that we are still immersed in the *absurdity of evil*. There are not just men and women of

good will who by chance, out of negligence or error have made some mistakes. The absurdity of evil, gratuitous evil, deliberate cruelty for the sake of it, the idol of success – these are all realities. The absurdity of Christ's cross is the result, and it is more relevant than ever.

While recognising so many noble pacifist efforts, we must never forget that this is the context we live in.

With this as our background we can continue meditating on the Our Father. Given that we are seeking God's will in our lives during this retreat, let us ask him: how do you want us to act in a world mired in conflict, a world troubled by such absurdity?

Asking for forgiveness

We have already, while meditating on the Our Father, considered that it is possible to refer to the *Principle and foundation* of the *Exercises*. I am now proposing to go to the First Week of the *Exercises*, the penitential week, the so-called purgative way in which we acknowledge our sins, the evil in us, our connivance with worldliness, our weaknesses, our fragility, in order to be purified.

St Ignatius proposes five meditations: the first on sins in the history of salvation, the second on personal sin, the third and fourth as repetitions of the first two to inscribe in the retreatant's heart what the Lord has had him understand; and the fifth is on damnation as sin's point of arrival.

We will allow ourselves to be guided by the spirit of this week, where we usually prepare for sacramental confession,

in such a way that we can experience it perhaps by looking back over the whole year that has passed since our last retreat.

The Our Father can help us. By reversing the order of the invocations we can dwell on the petition: "Forgive us our trespasses as we forgive those who trespass against us," and in the subsequent meditations on the words "and lead us not into temptation but deliver us from evil."

Perhaps we wonder why so much space is given to sin in the Our Father – out of seven petitions, *three* concern evil and sin.

Jesus knows our life is full of hidden dangers, is fragile and develops in a context of absurdity and sin, so is in constant need of being ransomed, defended from such circumstances.

Every community is also constantly mired in division, opposition, conflict. Jesus has us understand this. We often marvel at it because we have not understood the Our Father fully, while Jesus is not so amazed by it.

I recall the interesting title of a book by Jean Vanier: *La Communità luogo del perdono e della festa* (literally, Community, a place of forgiveness and celebration). Firstly of forgiveness insofar as the community is a place of sinfulness so we must insistently ask forgiveness for ourselves and forgive those who have offended us.

Let us tackle the petition: "Forgive us our trespasses as we forgive those who trespass against us."

It is a very important request, not only for the fact that we are constantly menaced by sin, but because Jesus' work,

the kingdom, is first of all about being freed from sin. This is how *Matthew's* Gospel presents him in the angel's revelation to Joseph: "She will bear a son, and you are to name him Jesus, for he will save his people from their sins" (1:21). Liberation from sin is an integral, substantial part of his mission. This is why he forgives our trespasses as we forgive those who trespass against us.

I propose we spend time with this petition of the Our Father, firstly with a *lectio* then by reflecting on the attitudes it suggests.

Freely offered forgiveness

Let us consider the words individually.

– *Luke* has the more usual wording: "forgive us our sins" (11:4); but *Matthew*, whose expression is the more archaic and primitive, as we have said, says: "forgive us our debts" (6:12) and that is not so common.

In the Hebrew Bible as in the Greek there are many terms to indicate sin, transgression, disobedience. Here he chooses the concept of debt and we ask why.

Probably because the idea of debt – obviously in a metaphorical sense insofar as we are not dealing with financial debt – is relational. Sin can be conceived of just by referring to the law: there is the law and sin transgresses the law: precept, and deviation from the precept. Instead here, debt points to a relationship with someone. By speaking of debts, then, Jesus reminds us that it is not simply a case of our deviations, transgressions, mistakes, infractions of the law but a breakdown of relationships with him.

82

In my opinion, therefore, this word is very important. It could also be correctly translated as "sin" but sin meaning a break in relationship with God.

– "*Forgive us* our debts": We confess we are unable to repay these debts. We could say: I have some debts and sooner or later I will repay them. But the debts we have with God we cannot repay.

Matthew expresses this clearly in the parable of the unforgiving servant:

> ".... the kingdom of heaven may be compared to a king who wished to settle accounts with his slaves. When he began the reckoning, one who owed him ten thousand talents was brought to him; and, as he could not pay, his Lord offered him to be sold, together with his wife and children and all his possessions, and payment to be made. So the slave fell on his knees before him, saying, 'Have patience with me, and I will pay you everything'. And out of pity for him, the Lord of that slave released him and forgave him the debt" (18:23-27).

The Lord first demanded that the slave be sold, and later accepted the pleas for mercy and forgave the debt.

The Our Father presumes this is how we are before God: we have debts we cannot pay because we have ruptured a relationship of love, and are unable to re-establish it of our own accord unless it is done for us, freely: "Forgive us our debts" is a truly central plea. We do not even know how much our debts are.

The parable speaks of ten thousand talents, but if we face up to what the Lord has done for us, the love he has embraced us with from all eternity, the fact that he has followed us, sought us out, sustained us, then our debt is incalculable, nor can it be resolved unless he makes some gesture of gratuity and forgives it.

Be perfect as the Father is perfect

"*As we also have forgiven our debtors*" (Mt 5:12). Luke picks up on the same word: "for we ourselves forgive everyone indebted to us."

Exegetes are surprised at the addition, noting that "forgive us our debts" is the only petition which is not a simple one. All the others are: hallowed be thy name, thy kingdom come, thy will be done, give us today our daily bread. The unified layout of the prayer is disturbed and exegetes ask themselves whether it departs from the original prayer as taught by Jesus. Yet everything makes us see that it is. Besides, it is the only petition which Jesus attaches a condition to and which directly calls on us to do something.

The Greek version has a very strange expression which exegetes discuss: "*os kai emeìas 'aphékamen' tois ophéletais emòm,*" "*as we have forgiven* our debtors."

It seems almost as if we have first had to forgive and then we can ask for forgiveness. It is true that exegetes usually soften this expression by saying that the perfect tense *'aphékamen'* is a perfect present, that is "*we are accustomed*

to forgive." But there is still a strict relationship between the two.

So what does this petition presume? It presumes a divided quarrelsome community where there is mutual offence, expectations not met, recriminations, disappointed hopes. And the petition is so strong that as I have already reminded you, the only commentary on the Our Father in the Sermon on the Mount is the one added immediately after the prayer: "For if you forgive others their trespasses, your heavenly Father will also forgive you; but if you do not forgive others, neither will your Father forgive your trespasses" (*Mt* 6:14-15). It is an absolute condition and stresses the fact that the Father well knows we are poor, fragile and easily offend one another. He wants to guarantee that his forgiveness is always accompanied by ours. As Jesus teaches us again in the parable in *Mt* 18, we who have received so much forgiveness from God are called on to make at least the gesture of forgiveness, forgiving others the little wrongs of theirs we have suffered.

"But that same slave, as he went out, came upon one of his fellow slaves who owed him a hundred denarii, and seizing him by the throat he said 'Pay what you owe". Then his fellow slave fell down and pleaded with him, 'Have patience with me and I will pay you'. But he refused; then he went and threw him into prison until he would pay the debt. When his fellow slaves saw what had happened, they were greatly distressed, and they went and reported

to their Lord all that had taken place. Then his Lord summoned him and said to him, 'you wicked slave! I forgave you all that debt because you pleaded with me. Should you not have had mercy on your fellow slave, as I had mercy on you? And in anger his Lord handed him over to be tortured until he would pay his entire debt. So my heavenly Father will also do to every one of you, if you do not forgive your brother or sister from your heart" (vv. 28-35).

It is certainly a very demanding petition. We Christian people often say it without really taking account of what it means. In fact it says so much: it commits us to freely offered forgiveness which is a huge, difficult and sometimes heroic gesture.

It commits us to an evangelical attitude which is by no means obvious. In the sermon on the Mount Jesus had already said:

> "So when you are offering your gift at the altar, if you remember that your brother or your sister has something against you leave your gift there before the altar and go; first be reconciled to your brother or sister and then come and offer your gift" (Mt 5:23-24).

These are fiery words which embarrass us every time we celebrate Eucharist, since we are never sure there is not someone with us with whom maybe we have not been able to take the step of reconciliation.

———

This requirement of Jesus is a daunting one. We might think: if someone has something against me, let him speak up. Instead the Lord wants us to do what is possible so the other will have nothing against us.

The following is also very demanding:

> You have heard that it was said, '*An eye for an eye and a tooth for a tooth*'. But I say to you, Do not resist an evildoer. But if anyone strikes you on the right cheek turn to the other also; and if anyone wants to sue you and take your cloak, give your cloak as well...

This is forgiveness.

> ... and if anyone forces you to go one mile, go also the second mile. Give to everyone who begs from you, and do not refuse anyone who wants to borrow from you.

> You have heard that it was said, '*you shall love your neighbour* and hate your enemy.' But I say to you: Love your enemies and pray for those who persecute you, so that you may be children of your Father in heaven; for he makes his sun rise on the evil and the good, and sends rain on the righteous and on the unrighteous (vv. 38-45).

We understand the motive for Jesus' insistence: because this is the way the Father acts. God is like this, and this is how he is glorified. "*Be perfect, therefore, as your heavenly Father is perfect*" (v.48).

There are people who have suffered some grave wrong, some profound injustice, who harbour rancour for years. The heroism of the Gospel is difficult, but to live it is possible. I knew an association in Israel which came into existence through the initiative of a Jewish mother whose young daughter, just 14 years old, was already taking part in peace protests. She was killed by a terrorist when 16 and after suffering so much, her mother said: My pain is so great that I need to understand other's pain.

This gave birth to an association of Jewish and Arab families who have had a relative, a brother, a child or father killed by terrorism or war. They meet to share each other's pain and journey together toward reconciliation.

It seems to be a path somewhat beyond this world. Yet even the experience I have had visiting prisons has convinced me that this rule of Jesus is capable of exercising its influence even in the Civil penal system which in all states today looks for forms of reconciliation, reparation, restitution, in order to go beyond purely vindictive and punitive justice. Otherwise evil increases, prison makes people worse by teaching them to commit even more evil. These approaches have already been realised, for example, in South Africa where a Truth, Peace and Reconciliation Commission was set up and fostered extraordinary gestures.

The Our Father's plea to "forgive us our trespasses as we forgive those who trespass against us" touches closely on all of us.

To sum up, what inner dispositions are implied?

Feeling that I am before the Father who loves me infinitely and wants to make me one with Jesus, wants to give

himself completely to me.

Considering my sins, faults, failures, inability to reciprocate love, love not given, not returned, not exchanged.

Praying in the plural, aligning myself with all sinners: "Forgive *us* our trespasses." Being in solidarity with the sins of the whole world.

And again, being ready to forgive with all my heart, and especially (even more difficult) to forgive whoever has not given me what I could have reasonably expected from them. This mindset also concerns families (parents-children, brothers and sisters), friendships and communities.

It is a typical evangelical teaching which we also find in the New Testament Epistles:

> Put away from you all bitterness and wrath
> and anger and wrangling and slander, together
> with all malice (*Eph* 4:31).

Bitterness: when I get upset with someone who has wronged me; wrath, because I was not given what I expected; anger, because I was not satisfied.

> ... and be kind to one another, tender-
> hearted, forgiving one another as God in Christ
> has forgiven you. Therefore be imitators of God
> as beloved children, and live in love as Christ
> loved us and gave himself up for us, a fragrant
> offering and sacrifice to God (4:32 - 5:2).

Other passages could be quoted which insist on this teaching.

It is interesting to note that *Mark*, while not giving us the Our Father, writes:

Whenever you stand praying, forgive, if you have anything against anyone; so that your Father in heaven may also forgive you your trespasses (11:25).

So the exhortation is found at all New Testament levels because it is absolutely characteristic of Jesus' message.

Praying in truth

Let us ask ourselves finally which attitudes the words of the Our Father suggest regarding our meditation.

– A first attitude, rarer than it should be, is *the certainty of being forgiven.*

Sometimes we drag ourselves through life preserving, despite many assurances, the fear that the Lord still has something against us. It is one of Satan's temptations. Once we have confessed our sins, God really does forgive us.

The New Testament often reminds us of this, for example in Col 1:13b-14:

(He has) transferred us into the kingdom of his beloved Son in whom we have redemption, the forgiveness of sins.

And in Eph 1:6-7:

.... to the praise of his glorious grace that he freely bestowed on us in the Beloved. In him we have redemption through his blood, the forgiveness of our trespasses, according to the riches of his grace.

We are invited to put our hearts at peace because God loves us and is at peace with us.

– A Second attitude is recommended and it is *the effort to eliminate all rancour,* all bitterness, any recriminations often hidden, even though they don't surface, in the depths of our psyche. We need to work hard at eliminating all this, listening once more to Jesus' words in the sermon on the Mount!

> Do not judge, so that you may not be judged. For with the judgement you make you will be judged and the measure you give will be the measure you get (*Mt* 7:1-2).

It asks of us that our judgement be good, kindly, while we may think we are good but retain the harshness of judgement which measures others with our strict measure.

– The third attitude is that of *entering into the Father's mercy. Luke* reminds us of this in a very effective way:

Be merciful, just as your Father is merciful.

> Do not judge, and you will not be judged; do not condemn and you will not be condemned. Forgive and you will be forgiven; give and it will be given to you. A good measure, pressed down, shaken together, running over will be put into your lap; for the measure you give will be the measure you get back. (6:36-38)

In other words: entering into the Father's mercy means loving ourselves as Jesus loved us (Cf. Jn 13:34-35).

Let us ask, through Mary's intercession, that these gospel sentiments may grow in us and express the newness of

life, the mutual leavening that allows us to be and remain together even though we are different and from different backgrounds.

"I WAS SENT FOR THIS PURPOSE"
(HOMILY)

It is God who waters and gives growth.

And so, brothers and sisters, I could not speak to you as spiritual people, but rather as people of the flesh, as infants in Christ. I fed you with milk, not solid food, for you were not ready for solid food. Even now you are still not ready, for you are still of the flesh. For as long as there is jealousy and quarrelling among you, are you not of the flesh, and behaving according to human inclination? For when one says, "I belong to Paul," and another "I belong to Apollos," are you not merely human?

What then is Apollos? What is Paul? Servants through whom you came to believe, as the Lord assigned to each. I planted, Apollos watered but God gave the growth. So neither the one who plants nor the one who waters is anything, but only God who gives the growth.

———

The one who plants and the one who waters have a common purpose, and each will receive wages according to the labour of each. For we are God's servants working together; you are God's field, God's building (1 Cor 3:1-9).

We ask ourselves what kind of language Paul uses when speaking to spiritual people if the pages of the First Letter to the Corinthians create so much difficulty for us, seem so high-flown, lofty, although Paul says they are still written for people of the flesh! It means there is still much to understand about the mystery of the kingdom of God and we are grateful to the Lord even if we can only grasp something of these words which are not yet the "solid food" of spiritual people according to the Apostle.

The first words we are invited to understand (we have already seen this in the morning meditation) is that there are divisions in the community. There were divisions in Paul's community involving some very holy people – Paul, Apollos, Cephas – so we should never be surprised.

I recall once giving a retreat on this theme: *Utopia on trial in a community*. I commented on the First Letter of the Corinthians, highlighting the relationship there between Paul's utopia, his ideal of community, and the reality of a community which knew of sexual abuse, the faithful split into opposing groups, abuses in cultural and Eucharistic assemblies.

It is clear that there can be a zealous, strong, spiritual, free Christianity – certainly the case for the primitive communities – but which is suffering at the same time.

It is something that surprises us and that we succeed in understanding and accepting only with time.

In the past I judged divisions within monasteries quite harshly, especially when some broke away to begin new experiences. To me it seemed too conflicted, not gospel-based. Then I became aware that much of the history of the great monasteries and religious orders was this way: divisions, conflicts, personalities, separations.

We are people of the flesh, we are weak: we need to take account of this and accept it without being scandalised.

This does not mean we should not try with all our strength to live in the fraternal communion Jesus spoke to us about and for which he prayed (Cf. *Jn* 17); but it is important to know that we are called to aim at unity in a community which will always have a degree of conflict in it. If we acknowledge it, blessed are we, and we should not be too afraid; we can act positively and purposefully. Learning that neither our efforts nor those of Apollos, Cephas, really count because it is *God who waters and gives growth.*

All that is good in our communities comes from the Father. We do some small service, maybe trampling on others' toes and with so much division and dissension, but it is He who works and saves.

It is admirable that the Lord saves us, starting from our poverty; even our sinfulness constantly calls us back to forgiveness ("forgive us our trespasses as we forgive those who trespass against us") despite not expecting an end to this journey because tomorrow we will need to be forgiven new trespasses and will have new trespasses to forgive.

97

This is the life of human beings which is thus perfected, purified, scoured. We need to grow in trust, mercy, our ability to read God's plan in the rather miserly, mean little efforts of our communities, and of ourselves.

A free and courageous ministry

After leaving the synagogue he entered Simon's house. Now Simon's mother-in-law was suffering from a high fever, and they asked him about her. Then he stood over her and rebuked the fever, and it left her. Immediately she got up and began to serve them.

As the sun was setting, all those who had any who were sick with various kinds of diseases brought them to him; and he laid his hands on each of them and cured them. Demons also came out of many, shouting, "you are the Son of God!" But he rebuked them and would not allow them to speak because they knew he was the Messiah.

At daybreak he departed and went into a deserted place. And the crowds were looking for him; and when they reached him, they wanted to prevent him from leaving them. But he said to them, "I must proclaim the good news of the kingdom of God to the other cities also; for I was sent for this purpose." So he continued

---

proclaiming the message in the synagogues of Judea (*Lk* 4:38-44).

The Gospel shows us Jesus at an exemplary moment of his life, one where he is planning ahead: he has compassion on the sick and heals them – Peter's mother-in-law and many others. He forbids the demons from speaking about him because testimony must come from the heart and from faith, not from someone who does not believe. At daybreak he withdraws to pray. I have always been amazed that while he mentions prayer so much, Luke does not say that Jesus withdrew to a deserted place to pray. *Mark* records this (Cf. 1:35), while *Luke* probably just presumes it.

In any case, we admire Jesus' gesture of freedom: the people are looking for him, want to detain him, want to possess him exclusively. Instead, he is for everyone, has a mission for everyone.

I would like to dwell for a moment on the words "for I was sent for this purpose," because that is where our strength lies. When we find ourselves faced with temptation, misunderstanding, humiliation, bitter moments, we need to say: "for I was sent for this purpose," it is here that I find myself as a priest, because through my suffering I share in Christ's suffering for the sake of his body which is the Church, as St Paul says (Cf. *Col* 1:24).

Let us thank the Lord for this sharing too in the sufferings of and for his Church.

1

MEDITATION
"LEAD US NOT INTO TEMPTATION"

Come, Holy Spirit, fill the hearts of your faithful and rekindle in them the fire of your love.

Remind us, divine Spirit, of what we said at the beginning: that these days are a ministry of the Spirit for us, because it is you who are at work in us. Grant that we may let ourselves be guided by you, your inspirations, consolations, but also by your silences. Grant that we may be fully prepared to accept the will of God which you want us to understand.

You see our weakness, mine in particular, in expressing this will. Grant that each of us receive from you the influence, strength, joy, clarity for accomplishing what is pleasing to God.

Mary, Mother of Jesus, Patroness of retreatants, assist us on this journey.

Sin, disorder, worldliness

In today's meditation I am offering some reflections on the petition "lead us not into temptation."

It is useful to recall that in the Ignatian *Exercises* the First Week, the week of purification, does not regard sin alone – hence it is worth recalling what we have already explained: in the Our Father we find the word "debt" in at least one of its versions, which places it within the framework of a personal relationship with the Father, Son and Holy Spirit.

St Ignatius does not only speak of purification from sins, but at no. 63 he asks for three graces in three important colloquies with Our Lady, Jesus , the Father. Let me read from the text:

> The first colloquy will be with our Blessed Lady, that she may obtain grace for me from her Son and Lord......:

> 1) A deep knowledge of my *sins* and a feeling of abhorrence for them;

This is the penitential way as we ordinarily describe it.

> 2) An understanding of the *disorder* of my actions, that filled with horror of them, I may amend my life and put it in order.

So Ignatius is inviting us to consider our life also from the point of view of my disorderly actions. Disorder is everything that without it necessarily being formal sin, especially serious sin, does not correspond to the end for which we were created, and as a consequence fills our life

with all kinds of disorderly, less than transparent behaviour. Disorder is the kind of activity in which we are led to pleasing ourselves, our comforts, tastes, wants, even though they do not reach the formal state of sinfulness.

> 3) A knowledge of the *world*, that filled with horror, I may put away from me all that is worldly and vain.....

Vanity is the shallow lifestyle which chases after success, good reputation, the approval of others. Without being formal sinfulness it nevertheless wrecks our interior life.

In the second and third colloquies we find "I will make the same petitions to her Son that He may obtain these graces from the Father for me," and "I will make the same requests of the Father that He himself, the eternal Lord, may grant them to me."

In examining ourselves, then, we should bear in mind both our formal sins and all the disorder and vanity which make up much of our daily life and are a burden to it, obscure it, make it less happy, more awkward, less enthusiastic, less generous.

All this is also relevant to the matter of temptations which have the effect of burdening our soul. After this we can reflect truly on the meaning of the petition in the Our Father: "Lead us not into temptation."

Why speak of temptation?

The petition is just a bit scandalous in the way it is worded. The Church has struggled for centuries against

---

the apparent scandalous nature of the wording and has constantly sought to re-express it in other ways.

St Ambrose, for example, translated it as: "*Do not allow us to fall into temptation.*" The prayer's "Do not lead us" is actually a harsh way to put it because it seems as if God is tempting us into evil. We know that the Italian Episcopal Conference did everything to try to change it in the new edition of the Bible, by replacing it with "Do not abandon us to temptation" in order to soften the expression somewhat.

In any case it is clear that the Our Father makes room for temptation and makes it the subject of a specific request. It could surprise us that after mentioning sins and mutual forgiveness, there is still a plea about being freed from temptation.

Temptation really is an important part of the Christian experience and in factual terms an almost daily experience.

Jesus warned us about it, telling the apostles: "Stay awake and pray that you may not come into the time of trial; the spirit indeed is willing but the flesh is weak" (*Mt* 26:41); he himself had been tempted by sadness and fear (Cf. vv 37-38).

He also sought to begin his public ministry by submitting himself in the desert to Satan's temptation, as the Synoptics recount: "Then Jesus was led up by the Spirit into the wilderness to be tempted by the devil" (*Mt* 4:1; Cf. *Mk* 1:12-13 and *Lk* 4:1-2). Then he was subjected to serious temptations like the one after Peter's confession when he even called him "Satan" (Cf. *Mt* 16:23 and *Mk* 8:36): Jesus felt that Peter's words ("God forbid it Lord! This must never happen to you") were a serious temptation.

Jesus alone speaks to Peter about temptation where he says: "Simon, Simon, listen! Satan has demanded to sift all of you," not only him but all of them, "like wheat," to try to shake them up strongly, cause them to be afraid; "but I have prayed for you that your own faith may not fail: and you, when once you have turned back, strengthen your brothers" (*Lk* 22:31-32). He foresees serious temptation for the apostles, a fall for Peter, saving his faith however, and then a reform and confirmation of his brothers.

If temptation is an important part of Christian life, let us try to understand what "lead us not into temptation" means, or "do not allow us to fall into temptation" or "do not abandon us to temptation."

Five types of temptation

First of all, it is clear that the "do not lead us" is not saying that God tempts us to evil but that he permits temptation as a part of our experience, that in some way it is necessary in order to grow in faith, hope and charity.

Naturally, it is a trap into which Satan the tempter does everything to make us fall. We are asking that we be freed from this trap which is very real and dangerous, even if we sidestep it, try to avoid it.

What temptation are we talking about?

Exegetes have discussed this at length. Those who interpret the Our Father in eschatological terms maintain that it is dealing with temptation *par excellence*, the eschatological kind regarding the end days which they

believe are nigh. The New Testament speaks of this. For example, we read in the *Second Letter to the Thessalonians*:

> And then the *lawless* one will be revealed, whom the Lord Jesus will *destroy with the breath of his mouth*, annihilating him by the manifestation of his coming. The coming of the lawless one is apparent in the working of Satan, who uses all power, signs, lying wonders, and every kind of wicked deception for those who are perishing, because they refused to love the truth and so be saved. For this reason God sends them a powerful delusion, leading them to believe what is false, so that all who have not believed the truth but took pleasure in unrighteousness will be condemned (2:8-12).

These are terrible words about the final temptation, Satan's last outbreak.

Matthew talks about it in the eschatological discourse: "And many false prophets will arise and lead many astray. And because of the increase of lawlessness, the love of many will grow cold: (24:11-12).

Truly this mysterious threat exists, which the faithful rightly ask to be freed from, preserved, saved, kept safe from.

Such an eschatological interpretation is no longer regarded as relevant today by many who refer the wording in the Our Father to temptations which make up the life of the believer; and they are many.

I will list five to help you reflect on the very many other temptations that can be relevant for each of us, according to the trials the Lord permits. I am thinking of *seduction, contradiction, self-deceit, God's silence, Jesus' insignificance.*

• *Seduction.* Seduction is attraction to evil – sensuality, envy, pride, excessive power, cruelty, revenge, violence, evil which presents as such (even though it is true that we always consent to evil because it appears to have some semblance of good).

Sometimes seduction is so strong that Satan seems to enter us, invading our psyche and body, when we risk behaving with a perversity that we never could have imagined. We need to know how to guard against it and that is relatively easy precisely because it is about evil: sensuality, disordered sexuality, pornography, envy, cursing, vengeance, insults, lies that cause serious harm, stealing and so forth. This is all part of human experience.

In *Mark's* Gospel we find a fine-tuned list of such departures from the norm of good behaviour. In my opinion it was a list that was a kind of compendium of moral theology for catechumens. They were invited to make an extensive examination of conscience and mention by name the faults and vices that most tempted them:

> When he had left the crowd and entered the house his disciples asked him about the parable. He said to them, "Then do you also fail to understand? Do you not see that whatever goes into a person from outside cannot defile; since it enters, not the heart but the stomach, and goes

out into the sewer?" (Thus he declared all foods clean). And he said, "It is what comes out of a person that defiles. For it is from within, from the human heart, that evil intentions come: fornication, theft, murder, adultery, avarice, wickedness, deceit, licentiousness, envy, slander, pride, folly. All these evil things come from within and they defile a person (7:17-23).

We are invited to question our own heart given that "these evil things" are all within us, including in our subconscious or unconscious, and often they do not emerge because the occasion has not arisen.

We can observe that nine of the intentions, nine forms of evil, are in three groups of three.

The clearest are the first three: fornication, theft, murder.

The three that come next are a bit more shadowy: adultery, avarice, wickedness.

Lying even deeper within the heart are deceit, licentiousness, envy.

Finally, slander, pride and folly are perhaps the most "ecclesiastical" because they often infest the Church's garden.

So these are the seductions. We need to be aware of them, reflect on them, because we are all subject to them.

• The second type of temptation is *contradiction*. It affects us when we are doing good but find ourselves in surroundings that are critical of us, hinder us, put a spoke in our wheels, take us for a ride or simply block us. It is then that we need much patience, perseverance and humility.

Often our temptations are really contradictions maybe even coming from the Christian community itself, from people we thought were closer to us, more attentive. Yet they seem not to understand and oppose us, mock and dampen our efforts.

• The Third type of temptation is *self-deceit*, doing something that looks good but from which no good comes.

This is perhaps the most frequent temptation for good people who serve God generously, because the devil tempts them by urging them, for example, to a life of penance, austerity, on the pretext of poverty, authenticity, sincerity, righteousness, and gets them to act in mistaken ways. They think they are of some importance but trample on the most common rules of upright living under the banner of purity, severity, evangelical radicalness, and they easily go astray.

The devil St Ignatius warns us, temps especially *sub specie boni*, under the appearance of good, urging us to always do better but ending up with a fistful of very little to show for it, creating a vacuum around us, destroying a community – all starting from apparently good intentions.

• The fourth temptation is very serious: *God's silence*, a silence that makes human beings ask: Why, Lord, do you hide yourself? Why do you not speak? It is the temptation of the Jewish people during the *Shoah*. Still today they ask: Why did God not intervene? It is the temptation that assails us every time we expect God to come and we feel alone, abandoned, deprived of the help we expect.

God's silence is also a temptation that affects people well-advanced along the spiritual journey.

• The final temptation, tied in a certain sense to the previous one, is of a social kind. I see it clearly in Israel where Christians are few and have no public profile, but it is also found in our own Western countries where Christianity has no social relevance or is losing it. It is the *insignificance of Jesus.*

If everything is built around economic, political, cultural parameters which take no account of Jesus, considering him to be at best a decoration on the Christmas tree; if the media and amusements, public life in general go on as if there were no God, many Christians yield to this strong temptation which has them living a double life: they pray in the parish but outside the parish Jesus might as well not exist.

On other occasions I have already spoken of the testimony of a German spiritual father who at his Golden Jubilee of Ordination replied to those who asked him about his priestly experience: the greatest trial over these fifty years for me was not the Second World War or Nazism but the fact that the people distanced themselves from the Church and even the most fervent Christian communities rapidly diminished to just a handful.

It is a trial we are asked to undergo because the Lord is present there too. It is a temptation that requires an increase in faith. This is why I have always insisted on the need to practice *lectio divina* which constantly regenerates our faith. If we have this inner wealth that the Word of God meditated upon day after day builds up and rebuilds, we can even face an army, even face complete isolation.

I would like to suggest that you read the First Letter of Peter to better understand how to overcome this pernicious

temptation which is the Christian feeling of being insignificant. It is a letter written to believers living in the diaspora and a situation of social marginalisation, and constantly tempted to say: we are poor creatures who count for nothing.

In a marvellous way, Peter rebuilds their price in being Christian, the joy of being so even in humiliation, insignificance, trial, suffering, showing them that it is in such circumstances that the Gospel is shown to be true, the kingdom comes, Jesus triumphs.

Avoiding occasions of temptation

I would like to add a further note on this reflection on the petition to "lead us not into temptation."

I think I could put it this way: just as forgiveness of sins ("Forgive us our trespasses") is tied to our forgiving each other for the wrongs done to us ("Forgive us our trespasses as we forgive those who trespass against us"), in the same way our defence against the enemy's trap which is temptation, is tied to avoiding occasions of temptation by virtue of Jesus' words. It is not said in the Our Father, but to me it seems to be implicit: "lead us not into temptation," so for our part we try to avoid the occasions of sin.

The idea is repeated at least twice, and strongly, in this context. First of all in the Sermon on the Mount:

> If your right eye causes you to sin, tear it out and throw it away: it is better for you to lose one of your members than for your whole body to be thrown into hell. And if you right

hand causes you to sin, cut it off and throw it away; it is better for you to lose one of your members than for your whole body to go into hell (*Mt* 5:29-30).

The context is one of adultery and the sanctity of married life: "... everyone who looks at a woman with lust has already committed adultery with her in his heart" (v. 27).

It is clear that this is presenting the radical requirement to avoid temptation, so it can easily be linked to the request to "lead us not into temptation."

The words return as such in the so-called discourse on the Church in Ch. 18 where *Matthew* says:

If your hand or foot causes you to stumble, cut it off and throw it away: it is better for you to enter life maimed or lame than to have two hands or two feet and to be thrown into the eternal fire. And if your eye causes you to stumble, tear it out and throw it away: it is better for you to enter life with one eye than to have two eyes and to be thrown into the hell of fire (vv. 8-9).

It is one of the very rare occasions where the same sentence is repeated in identical terms twice in two different places in the same Gospel. This means it is of great importance to Jesus and the primitive preaching. And if the first context is one of adultery the sanctity of marriage, the second is that of scandal, scandalising the little ones. Immediately preceding it are the words:

Whoever welcomes one such child in my name welcomes me. If any of you put a stumbling block before one of these little ones who believe in me, it would be better for you if a great millstone were fastened around your neck and you were drowned in the depths of the sea (vv. 5-6).

These are very harsh words. Perhaps they seem a bit abstract reading them but they are very realistic, very relevant; we think for example of so many scandals over recent years, of cases of paedophilia.

Lord Jesus, you scrutinise our hearts and know our fragility and weaknesses. Sustain us in the trials we meet along the journey of faith.

We know well that with your help we can resist temptation. Grant that we may always believe that you are near us so we do not feel alone and will persevere in hope.

Grant that the certainty that God is faithful, as Paul teaches us (Cf. 1 Cor 10:13) may never diminish in us; the certainty that he will not allow us to be tempted beyond our strength if, like children, we abandon ourselves trustingly into the Father's hands.

2

MEDITATION
"BUT DELIVER US FROM EVIL"

No one knows the Son except the Father,
and no one knows the Father except the Son and
anyone to whom the Son chooses to reveal him
(*Mt* 11:27).

These words invite us to pray:

*Grant that your Son Jesus be make known to us, Father. We
seek to get to know him through the Our Father he taught us,
because we are sure that he put his whole heart into this prayer,
everything he had at heart, everything that was important to
him and which he wanted to pass on to us. Father, grant that
we may come to know his intimate awareness, so that we can
be enlightened, our doubts clarified and we can be inwardly
ordered. We also ask you, Father, through your Son, that we
may know you since no one knows you unless the Son reveals
you. May he reveal you also through this prayer.*

*Grant that we may come to know your will for us, and that
we may accept and embrace it, embrace our crosses whatever
they may be because they come from your loving plan for us.*

May Mary intercede for us as our Mother and Mother of the Church. She abandoned herself to the Father's will in these words: Father, let it be with me according to your word.

Grant that we may join with Mary in her dedication to your will, to find in it the fullness of joy for ourselves and for the world. Amen.

"Tear us away" from sinfulness

In this meditation we will be reflecting on the petition "But deliver us from evil." According to Fr Ledrus, to understand the Our Father it is pedagogically better to begin from the final petition because it is the one we have the most experience of; even though ontologically and from a values perspective, the Our Father has a structure that begins from above and descends from there, from God's name to evil.

I will first of all offer a *lectio*, word by word, then we will make a *meditatio* in the effort to reply to two questions: how do wickedness and the Evil one go to work on us? How can we resist the Evil one?

• The words "but deliver us from evil," as we know, are not found in Luke. The welter of exegetical interpretations starts here: did Luke leave it out or did Matthew add it? And why does it start with a "but"?

Clearly the "but" is *explanatory*, not adversative, since the request to "lead us not into temptation" is in the negative, while "deliver us from evil" is in the positive, and the two requests are linked with a "but".

However, a further question arises: is "deliver us from evil" simply another way of saying "lead us not into

temptation"? Is it a synonymous parallelism, or does it add something, almost as a summary conclusion to the Our Father?

One indication might come from considering the word "deliver".

- *"Deliver us."* The Greek verb (*rysai*) is more eloquent because it means *"tear us away from"* evil. It provides us with the image of someone who is being gnawed by a lion, for example, and who is ripped away from its jaws.

John the Evangelist is certainly more bland when he gives us Jesus' splendid prayer to the Father and uses a softer word: "I am not asking you to *take them out of* (àres) the world but I ask you to protect them from the Evil one" (17:5) as if the enemy's assault has still not taken place. This could almost be paraphrased as: "do not let them fall into temptation." Instead "deliver us, tear us away" from evil is a cry which presumes we are already in the lion's fangs.

We find the more dramatic use of the verb *ryomai* in Mt 27:43. Jesus is on the cross: "He trust in God; let God *deliver him* now, if he wants to." Jesus is already on the cross and to "deliver" him means to take him off, pull him off the cross.

We find another occurrence of this verb in the *Benedictus*:

> Thus he has *shown the mercy promised to our ancestors, and has remembered his holy covenant, the oath that he swore* to our ancestor *Abraham*, to grant us that we, *being rescued from* (*rysthéntas*) the hands of our enemies might serve him

without fear, in holiness and righteousness before him all our days (*Lk* 1:73-74).

This tells us that our enemies are not just a distant threat but we are already in their hands.

Again there is Paul's dramatic exclamation in the *Letter to the Romans*: "Wretched man that I am! Who *will rescue me* (*rysetai*) from this body of death?" (7:24). I am in a body that carries me toward death, sin, degradation; I have to be torn away from it.

It seems to me, then that the words "deliver us" add something by comparison with the request to "lead us not into temptation": we can be preserved from temptation but when we are in the clutches of Satan we need to be torn away, freed from the wickedness surrounding us on all sides seducing, involving and overwhelming us. It is a truly heartfelt cry and echoes the Psalmists. I am thinking of the psalms concerning the sick, the prisoner, the vanquished who ask to be pulled out of the ditch, not be left as prey for the enemy.

This is the meaning of the verb "deliver us".

The other item is "*from evil*," *apò tou poneroù.*

First of all, this is not alluding to philosophical evil, abstract evil (*kakòn*), hard to define. *Apò tou poneroù* refers to being freed from nastiness, from what is evil. It can be thought of as both masculine and neuter: from evil, from the evil one, but also from nastiness, wickedness.

Over the long history of the Church we have always asked ourselves: do we need to say "deliver us from evil" or "deliver us from the Evil one"?

The Italian Bishops Conference, for its new translation of the Bible, chose a middle way after much to-ing and fro-ing, whereby *"Male"* (Evil) was written with a capital M ("deliver us from Evil"), thus including both meanings.

But the problem remains.

There are various examples in the New Testament of the word used in the neuter (*to poneròn*). One especially eloquent example is in the *Letter to the Romans*: "Let love be genuine. Hate what is *evil* (*to poneròn*), hold fast to what is good" (12:9). The good-evil opposition is clear and indicates that *to poneròn* is to be understood in the sense of wickedness, loathsomeness. These certainly have a mysterious, obscure reference (Satan the adversary) but it is not easy to distinguish it from the wickedness that has been introduced into the world and operates dynamically, involving us. There are so many similar cases in the New Testament and we could suppose, therefore, that the *tou poneroù* of the Our Father is neuter.

But it could also be thought of as masculine, and being in the singular could clearly only be applied to Satan. Sometimes in the New Testament we find it in the plural, which makes the masculine interpretation clearer – "deliver us from evil men."

Also interesting are some verses from the *Second Letter to the Thessalonians*:

> Finally, brothers and sisters, pray for us, so that the word of the Lord may spread rapidly and be glorified everywhere, just as it *is among you* and that we may be *rescued from* (*rysthòmen*)

wicked and evil people (*apò ton atòpon kai poneròn anthròpon*); for not all have faith. But the Lord is faithful; he will strengthen you and guard you from the evil one (*apò tou poneroù* (3:1-3).

It is possible that here it is a reference to Satan, the Evil one.

The answer to the question remains uncertain. For my part I maintain that it is much more probable to think first of all of the forces of evil, perhaps sown by Satan, but which by now are an avalanche enveloping the world. How could we not think of certain scenes during occupation, wars in other continents, the mass rapes in Bosnia, the atrocious actions of Chechen terrorists over recent days? This is the desire to perpetrate evil. It is pure wickedness, cruelty.

However, there is another hypothesis which seems to me to be an interesting one and it comes from Fr Ledrus who writes in his booklet:

> The "evil" we ask God to tear us away from is understood in all its breadth: moral evil, sin, the Evil one... The supreme evil, both in time and eternity, is a bad conscience. In itself bad conscience is rightly immanent, very just punishment: self-damnation, apostasy, alienation from God the supreme good, the devil taking up residence in the soul as its own temple (*op. cit.* p. 43).

This interpretation both amazes and attracts me. By "evil" he means a bad conscience, the taste for being immersed in wickedness, drawing up plans to make it ever more pervasive. This bad conscience is already punishment in itself because it gnaws away, unsettles, makes us neurotic and crazy. Nor is it so rare. There are people, even within the Christian religious context, who have allowed themselves to be so eaten up with rancour, disgust, scepticism that they have gained a taste for evil and, for example, find satisfaction in writing anonymous letters, denouncing people, ruining people's reputation.

Fr Ledrus says: "Do not say: deliver us from 'evils' because properly speaking there is only *one* evil, *damnation*, the final apostasy of children from their Father" (*ibid*).

We see it when we contemplate Jesus' passion. Some theologians maintain that when he cries out "My God, my God, Why have you forsaken me?" he touched the depths of evil and entered a situation similar to that of the damned who have separated themselves from God. One can also be "damned" in this life, in the sense of being totally alienated from him. And Fr Ledrus continues:

> Other evils are relative; even the sin we can eventually call "O felix culpa." But damnation does only one thing with everything that is part of it or leads to it; and in this sense all the evils of man form a block here since they come from sin and express the verdict which weighs on all of humanity (*ibid* pp. 43-44).

It is something similar to what some do, interpreting the "evil" at the conclusion of the Our Father as the opposite to the first part of the prayer: God is not made holy, the kingdom does not come, God's will is not done. Again:

> The evil, then, which this request speaks of, does not properly refer to sin committed. From sin committed we are freed, justified by divine forgiveness we pleaded for in the fifth request, "forgive us our trespasses." The seventh request refers practically speaking to *sinfulness*, that which leads us to sin, malice, corruption of the "rotten tree" on which only false fruits, wicked deeds can grow... hence here we are asking for liberation, salvation from the enmity of the devil, not in isolation from but considered together with the other two enemies of our salvation: the "world" and the "flesh", the devil's acolytes (ibid p.44).

These are efforts to fully understand the mysterious meaning of the word "evil" which attest to the richness and fundamental importance it has for our experience.

The wiles of the Evil one

During our *meditatio* we will attempt to reply to the questions: how does the Evil one (understood both as Satan and the Wickedness coming from him) work? And how do we resist the evil one or, how does the good spirit work in us?

In reference to this I would like to recall the rules for the discernment of spirits found in St Ignatius of Loyola's *Spiritual Exercises* and offer a brief summary of them. He offers them to the retreatants to teach them to discern their own inner movements, So by distinguishing which are the suggestions of the enemy from the suggestions of the Spirit they will be able to understand God's will for themselves and fulfil it. These rules, then are very valuable for someone on a spiritual journey.

The Evil one operates in four ways especially.

– Firstly by *seducing*. In the first rule St Ignatius writes: "... the enemy is ordinarily accustomed to propose apparent pleasures. He fills their imagination with sensual delights and gratifications, the more readily to keep them in their vices and increase the number of their sin" (no. 314).

I can add that seduction is often bound up with self-deception. Let us recall the example of a frequent behaviour today: I spend the evening watching television, go onto the internet to find pornographic programs and say to myself – I am not doing this out of my own sensuality but because I want to understand the kind of images our young people see. The motive is an apparently good one and Satan seduces us with this thought since he usually gets us involved and overwhelmed with apparent reasons. We already pointed to this when speaking about the first kind of temptation, seduction.

– Above all, whoever walks the way of truth and the Gospel is attached with sadness by the Evil one. "Then it is characteristic of the evil spirit to harass with anxiety, to

afflict with sadness, to raise obstacles backed by fallacious reasonings that disturb the soul. Thus he seeks to prevent the soul from advancing." (no. 315), suggesting we are incapable, that it is all too much for us, that we can't do it. It is the ordinary way the Evil one behaves with anyone seeking to keep to the right path and live the Gospel: he *saddens* us by making us lose courage, by bringing us down, infusing sorrow and melancholy.

St Ignatius describes this spiritual desolation as well, as it darkens the soul, tips it toward base and earthly things – almost a taste of sensuality, he unsettles the soul with various kinds of agitation and temptations – loss of points of reference, confusion, disorder, renders it distrustful, without hope, love, where it is lazy, lukewarm and separated from its Creator and Lord (Cf. no. 317). It is the typical activity of the spirit of evil upsetting us. It is absolutely essential to know how to recognise it and call it by name.

– Another activity of the spirit of evil is *to frighten.* Ignatius writes in Rule 12: "...the enemy becomes weak, loses courage, and turns to flight with his seductions as soon as one leading a spiritual life faces his temptations boldly, and does exactly the opposite of what he suggests. However, if one begins to be afraid and to lose courage in temptations, no wild animal on earth can be more fierce than the enemy of our human nature. He will carry out his perverse intentions with consummate malice" (no. 325).

When someone is frightened, hesitant, uncertain, he will be easily overwhelmed by the devil.

– The spirit of evil then, seduces, saddens, scares. Furthermore it *conceals, hides.* "... when the enemy of our human nature tempts a just soul with his wiles and seductions, he earnestly desires that they be received secretly and kept secret. But if one manifests them to a confessor, or to some other spiritual person who understands his deceits and malicious designs, the evil one is very much vexed. For he knows that he cannot succeed in his evil undertaking, once his evident deceits have been revealed" (no. 326).

It is not by chance that I always advise young priests especially to confide in someone, telling them of their passions, emotions, confusion, since this helps them to be clear about things.

– I will add a fifth way in which the Evil one acts: the enemy, *rides astride our physical and psychological weaknesses,* so we need to be very careful.

It is Satan's work to get us to say: let's go to bed as late as possible. This way he can take advantage of our physical tiredness, our nervous state, our irritation and especially any kind of depression or mental emptiness. When he sees we are depressed, he jumps on us and overwhelms us.

Therefore we need to understand the language of our body and bear well in mind that when we are tired, anxious, upset, somewhat exhausted or bewildered, we ought not follow our inclinations and thoughts because they could be negative and wayward.

With the help of St Ignatius' rules we have tried to describe some of the ways the Evil one acts in us.

Resisting the Evil one

We are allied with the Spirit of God, the Holy Spirit and the Church's tradition. If we did not have these allies we would be lost. Hence it is very necessary to know how to recognise the action of the good Spirit in us.

I will offer you two rules for this.

– We need to *listen to the Spirit who consoles.*

St Ignatius says in his second rule: "It is characteristic of the good spirit, however, to give courage and strength, consolations, tears, inspirations, and peace. This he does by making all easy, by removing all obstacles, so that the soul goes forward in doing good" (no. 315). Serenity and ease of action flow from this positive strength. The angel of darkness whispers to us: how can we remove the stone from the mouth of the tomb? How will we do it if the soldiers do not help us? But all of a sudden the good angel comes and the stone is rolled away.

Again, it is precisely the action of our ally in doing good that produces in us "an interior movement (is) aroused in the soul, by which it is inflamed with love of its Creator and Lord, and as a consequence, can love no creature on the face of the earth for its own sake, but only in the Creator of them all" (no. 316). This is the so-called *spiritual consolation,* the help God gives us to defeat Satan. "I call consolation every increase of faith, hope, and love, and all interior joy that invites and attracts to what is heavenly and to the salvation of one's soul by filling it with peace and quiet in its Creator and Lord" (*ibid*).

Everything that provides relief, ease, serenity, which resolves problems, is the work of the good Spirit.

We ought always remember that our existence is typified by the atmosphere of conflict we are immersed in. It is no peaceful, evolving journey from good to better. It is a struggle and it is of fundamental importance to know what its components are.

– Secondly, *the good spirit invites us to resist.*

It is essential, in difficult moments, to stand firm: "In time of desolation we should never make any change but remain firm and constant in the resolution and decision which guided us the day before the desolation, or in the decision to which we adhered in the preceding consolation" (no. 318).

Unfortunately we often make decisions at a time of confusion, disturbance, acrimony, and they are mistaken ones: "For just as in consolation the good spirit guides and counsels us, so in desolation the evil spirit guides and counsels. Following his counsels we can never find the way to a right decision" (*ibid*).

These words should be written clearly in the depths of our heart: I, we, have the grace to resist temptation, the evil spirit, with God's help.

I will finish by stressing the fact that a realistic, not an idyllic notion of reality makes us understand how immersed we are in the mystery of evil, which is not explained solely by our fragility or human weakness, our errors. It is the taste for doing wrong, making others suffer; it is pure

wickedness. We do not know how to explain it directly just because evil is absurd – we indicated this when speaking of the evil surrounding us and which we need to bear in mind over these days of retreat.

Perhaps we can understand something of this mystery by contemplating Christ's cross, by looking at the crucifix. We can surmise at least a little of the enormity and perversity of the deviations of every kind oppressing the world and can say: Lord Jesus, you conquered, overcame all this wickedness, and we are certain that with your grace we too will be able to conquer and overcome them!

UNLIMITED FAITH
IN THE WORD
(HOMILY)

A personal testimony

Once while Jesus was standing beside the lake of Gennesaret, and the crowd was pressing in on him to hear the Word of God, he saw two boats there at the shore of the lake; the fishermen had gone out of them and were washing their nets. He got into one of the boats, the one belonging to Simon, and asked him to put out a little way from the shore. Then he sat down and taught the crowds from the boat. When he had finished speaking, he said to Simon, "Put out into the deep water and let down your nets for a catch." Simon answered, "Master, we have worked all night long but have caught nothing, yet if you say so, I will let down the nets." When they had done this, they caught so many fish that their nets were beginning to break. So they signalled their partners in the other boat to come and help

---

them. And they came and filled both boats, so that they began to sink. But when Simon Peter saw it, he fell down at Jesus' knees saying, "go away from me, Lord, for I am a sinful man!" For he and all who were with him were amazed at the catch of fish that they had taken; and so also were James and John, sons of Zebedee, who were partners with Simon. Then Jesus said to Simon, "Do not be afraid; from now on you will be catching people." When they had brought their boats ashore, they left everything and followed him (*Lk* 5:1-11).

I am allowing myself a little bit of autobiography in this homily, because I have a very special rapport with today's Gospel passage. It was a passage proclaimed in the Sunday liturgy for the 5th Sunday of the year in 1980, the Sunday I celebrated Mass for the first time in the Cathedral in Milan, making my entrance to the diocese as Archbishop.

I saw myself in this passage, and saw in the crowd "pressing in" on Jesus the very many people filling the Cathedral – some 10,000 of them – and packing the Square outside.

Above all, like Simon, I felt my inadequacy: "Lord, I am not capable. I have laboured all night and caught very little." I experienced Peter's situation, humiliated and inadequate as he felt, as being mine. And I also perceived that I had to trust in Jesus' word, making it my policy, my programme.

"If you say so," so trusting in this word, proclaiming it, explaining it. Furthermore the passage begins by

emphasising that Jesus was preaching the word of God, and all the rest as a whole exalts the Word, the Word of God preached by Jesus and the word Jesus gave Peter: "Put out into deep water and let down your nets".

For me, putting out into deep water meant coming to a function of which I had no experience, coming into contact with a totally new world; it meant something like going form the earth to the moon, that is, from a service of an institutional, academic, scientific kind of pastoral service, starting out again from zero, knowing nothing and nobody. It really was a case of trusting only in Jesus' word.

I noted that this trust was given me as God's grace.

It was not in me, nor did I draw it out of some ministerial experience, which I was lacking. I had not the least idea what a diocese was all about, had not studied much Canon Law because I had dedicated myself mostly to the study of Holy Scripture. I did not know what a Curia was, for example, or what the function of a Vicar General was! And it was all given to me, placed in my hands with just one assurance: put out into the deep, and let down your nets for a catch.

I have experienced the truth of Jesus' words year by year and have always seen the beauty of the adventure I was living, and of trusting in him. Although my negligence and lack of accomplishments are plenty, just the same it seems to me that the nets have been full of fish, an enormous, unexpected amount, the nets almost breaking.

The fear of being inadequate grew on me little by little and I said, "Lord, why are you giving me this? Go away from me because I am a sinful man!"

———

Astonishment, fear, a sense of unworthiness, yet the Lord was always telling me: "Do not be afraid, from now on you will be catching people."

This text returns once a year in the weekday liturgy and twice when Luke's Gospel is read in the Sunday liturgy. And for the 22 years and 5 months I have served the Church of Milan, I have experienced the same sentiments.

"All things are yours"

Do not deceive yourselves. If you think that you are wise in this age, you should become fools so that you may become wise. For the wisdom of this world is foolishness with God. For it is written,

"He catches the wise in their craftiness, "

and again,

"The Lord knows the thoughts of the wise, that they are futile."

So let no one boast about human leaders. For all things are yours, whether Paul or Apollos or Cephas or the world or life or death or the present or the future – all belong to you, and you belong to Christ, and Christ belongs to God (1Cor 3:18-23).

I would also like to say something about the first Reading where St Paul disabuses us of the belief that there is finally a language that can be understood by the wisdom of this world.

We often accuse ourselves, complaining: we do not have the right words; if we had the language, the people would understand us, would follow us.

I never really believed much in the grasp we have of language.

It is true that when speaking, we should avoid everything that is archaic, unnatural, bureaucratic, theoretical. Just the same, when we speak as we live, there is little more we can do.

There is nothing that can build communication bridges unless we put aside our human self-sufficiency, a certain human wisdom. Accepting Jesus' humility will always require a leap in quality on our part, but we would do it in a way that Jesus' humility pleases and becomes something the world desires.

And it is right that it be so. God "Catches the wise in their craftiness," plays with them.

But when we have understood that the thoughts of the wise are futile, then we place all our trust in the Word and it is the Word that saves us and others.

Paul's text ends with a very beautiful sentence: "all belongs to you." - you are rich and free - "Paul or Apollos or Cephas or the world or life, or death or the present or the future" - we lose nothing when we belong to Christ, "and you belong to Christ, and Christ belongs to God."

So many problems regarding the Church too, its structures, its renewal, pale before this truth: that all belong to Christ and that Christ belongs to God, and God brings everyone and everything home. How, only he knows; but he is doing so and we are simple collaborators abandoned to his action, his power, the grace of his Spirit.

Let us ask, through the intercession of Mary, that we may live in trust and abandonment.

1

Meditation
"THY KINGDOM COME"

We have reached the culminating point of our retreat, the central petition of the Our Father: "Thy kingdom come." Until now we have been skirting around it somewhat, as if afraid to tackle it. Two verses from *Lk* 12 immediately spring to mind: "Instead, strive for his kingdom, and these things will be given to you as well. Do not be afraid, little flock, for it is your Father's good pleasure to give you the kingdom" (vv. 31-32).

We thank you, Father, because you were pleased to give us your kingdom. We are a small, insignificant flock compared to the clamour of our world, its dizzying power, its violence, its boasts of even more advanced scientific discoveries. We thank you because you gave the kingdom to us who are of so little importance and oft times marginalised. You invite us to seek it and ask for it. Grant, then, that we may understand what it consists of. It certainly corresponds to the most profound desire of your Son, Jesus. Grant that we may enter his heart to understand this kingdom and so journey toward it, allowing it a place in our hearts and lives. We ask you this, Father, through Christ our Lord.

―――――

The petition "Thy kingdom come" is the only real request, according to some exegetes. All the others act as a lead up to it. After reflecting on it at length I prefer the solution put forward by Fr Ledrus: "Hallowed be thy name" is the more radical, metaphysical appeal, while "Thy kingdom come" brings this about in history. "Hallowed be thy name: is the more general request, the more fundamental one, while "Thy kingdom come" refers to its embodiment in Jesus' life.

It is still difficult, naturally, to understand *what we are asking for* with the words "thy kingdom come."

St Ignatius of Loyola begins the Second Week of his *Spiritual Exercises* with a presentation of the kingdom; we could even look at this moment of our retreat as passing from the First to the Second Week. This is preceded by contemplation of the King and the kingdom, a preparatory and introductory meditation which Ignatius places at the beginning of the meditations on the life of Jesus, as a synopsis and key to interpretation.

> ...consider the address this king makes to all his subjects, with the words: "It is my will to conquer all the lands of the infidel. Therefore, whoever wishes to join with me in this enterprise must be content with the same food, drink, clothing, etc as mine. So, too, he must work with me day by day, and watch with me by night, etc, that as he has had a share in the toil with me, afterwards he may share in the victory with me (no.93).

This concept of the kingdom is obviously in the conquering style of the century Ignatius lived in: it sought submission of infidels to God's power.

It is not a mistaken view but it still leaves the question open: *How does the kingdom come?* Does it come through a power which destroys its enemies and conquers them in battle, as they thought at the time of the Crusades? Or is it something rather more akin to a seed, yeast, patient penetration of the mass?

The petition "Thy kingdom come," in my opinion, is open to so many different interpretations.

I would like to attempt an exploration, spelling it out in four considerations: the question as to what the kingdom is; the acknowledgement that the kingdom is not yet in place, yet it is coming; and finally, reflection on the attitudes with which we ask for the kingdom to come.

What is the Kingdom?

It is obvious, especially for the Synoptics, that the kingdom of God is Jesus' central concern, the condensed form of all his preaching, as we read from the beginning of Mark's account:

> Now after John was arrested, Jesus came to Galilee, proclaiming the good news of God, and saying, "The time is fulfilled, and the kingdom of God has come near; repent, and believe in the good news" (1: 14-15).

So the kingdom of God is at the centre of Jesus' proclamation.

• *Jesus, "definitions"*. The synoptics show Jesus speaking about the kingdom in many ways, especially in the parables, for example in Mk 4:26: "The kingdom of God is as if someone would scatter seed on the ground," and in Mk 4:30: "With what can we compare the kingdom of God, or what parable will we use for it?" At the beginning of the chapter the Evangelist has already, without speaking immediately of the kingdom, placed the best known parable, the sower, which is also a parable of the kingdom (Cf. vv. 2-9).

So Jesus speaks often about the kingdom but in parables, comparisons, through metaphors, allusions, images, without even giving a definition.

It is not easy to provide a synopsis of all that. To do so we need to unify the many mentions of the kingdom.

• *Attempts at a synopsis*. In my view we read the best synopsis in a note in the Jerusalem Bible on *Mt* 4:17: "The sovereignty of God over the Chosen People and through them over the world, is at the heart of Christ's preaching, as it was in the theocractic ideal of the Old Testament. It implies a kingdom of 'saints' where God will be truly king because they will acknowledge his royal rights by knowing and loving him. This sovereignty, jeopardised by rebellious sin, is to be reasserted by an act of supreme intervention on the part of God and of his Messiah. This is the interpretation which Jesus realises a successful nationalist uprising" [as we could expect from Ignatius parable] "but of a purely spiritual

movement. The redemptive work of Jesus as 'Son of Man' and as 'servant' sets man free form Satan's rule which opposes God's. Before it achieves its final eschatological realisation when the elect will be with the Father in the joy of the heavenly banquet, the kingdom makes an unimpressive entrance. Its modest beginning is mysterious and arouses opposition, it has come unnoticed" (we do not know how the seed tossed to the ground grows); "the development of the kingdom on earth is slow and is effected by the Church. By the judgement of God that falls upon Jerusalem it is established with power preached throughout the world by apostolic missionaries. When the time comes for the final judgement, the return of Christ in glory will be the final act which establishes the kingdom which Christ will then present to the Father. Until that time the kingdom appears as a free gift of God accepted by the humble and the generous, refused by the proud and selfish. There is no entering it without the wedding garment which is the new life. One must stay awake so as to be ready when it comes unexpectedly."

This is certainly a digest of many of the passages in the Synoptics, giving us to understand that the reality of the kingdom is not an easy one. It is complex, with modest beginnings, and is not advanced through force of arms and conquest, does not hinge on human power, but is above all a reality which enters hearts and is to be accepted by them.

The most eloquent and beautiful words on this I will read once more from Fr Ledrus' text:

The elementary truth is that God rules his entire creation from the beginning, unconditionally, including the part of creation that is free. [meaning God is always king] However, speaking now of 'kingdom' in the gospel sense, God reins when his goodness wins over, over the humble and spontaneous adherence of free hearts through gentle grace. Divine omnipotence is resplendent and sovereign in the triumphs of mercy when it brings eternal life in the elect to maturity; when it shows forbearance by sparing the darnel of scandal sown amidst the good seed of the word [not pulling it out by force], when it transforms the stumbling block, the relative success of evil, Calvary, into a 'corner-stone' for the living abode of adopted children. The gospel kingdom of the Father of mercies, then, is not reduced to God's effective ownership which also includes the damned under his power. The kingdom of Christ consists of the full and free effusion of divine life in and from the hearts of redeemed human beings (*op. cit.,* pp. 98-99).

This passage effectively emphasises the freedom, spontaneity, gradualness and gentleness of the kingdom. Continuing, he says:

This kingdom... is no less than the apostolic work of the Holy Spirit, considered in terms of its spread, and especially the heavenly

ordering of Christian life as the universal event of glorious eternity. The "Thy kingdom come" is a petition inspired by the concern that the already begun kingdom will develop; that it will be realised as first fruits in this life and as fulfilment in the final raising up. [This kingdom,] this powerful, manifest and victorious life of Christ in his followers is the mysterious, most solid and imposing reality to unfold in the universe; the most impenetrable, memorable, unforgettable fact of history: the kingdom begun, the kingdom in movement, the king living in the kingdom (ibid. pp. 9-100).

It is wonderful to see how all the above shows how rich this concept is and how widespread it is throughout the Gospels.

• *A reality understood through following Jesus.* We have already said that Jesus never sought to provide a brief summary of the nature of the kingdom; he always presented parables, indications about attitudes (such as the beatitudes), ethical, moral, theological indicators to get us to understand something which cannot be easily put into theological order but which is *understood by someone who lives it.*

The petition "Thy kingdom come" states this disciple's humble wish that something which is poor, meek, almost despised at the beginning will gradually conquer people's hearts and be joyfully and freely accepted.

This is the greatness of the kingdom, all balancing on freedom, meekness, spontaneity, persuasion; and it is its

weakness because it is not entrusted to a Power, an army, the ability to control human consensus either by force of arms, economic power, intellectual or political power. It is an intimate reality of the heart which nevertheless conquers the universe through the change of life it produces-we think of beatitudes which are the typical expression of the kingdom's life style.

At this point you are able to appreciate that I am embarrassed in not being able to offer a precise definition. I am trying to get there through various quotations and especially by calling on the Holy Spirit to grant us a profound understanding of the Gospels in such a way that it allows us to grasp the correct meaning of the kingdom as presented in the Sermon on the Mount, in the parables, the missionary discourse and so many of Jesus' other sayings.

The kingdom, then, is something that cannot be easily labelled, but is *experienced by following Jesus day by day* and trusting in the words of his Gospel. It is something that is experienced by setting out to follow Jesus who, from the outset of his public mission at the Jordan, humbles himself by joining the queue of sinners, and declaring that he wants to proclaim the kingdom in humility, hiddenness, despising privilege.

It is right to ask, therefore, that the kingdom come, because it cannot be one of our conquests. It is God who runs the kingdom, He who enters hearts and wins them over; it is He, by the grace of the Holy Spirit, who takes possession of souls and transforms them into the image of Jesus. In other words, *the kingdom is Jesus*, his life, his way

of living, loving, suffering. It is precisely because of this that it is proposed in a redoubtable and incontrovertible way in the cross, in Jesus' death out of love.

"Thy kingdom come" is a very elevated plea and perhaps we should say as Jesus told his disciples one day: "You do not know what you are asking" (*Mt* 20:22). We ask by intuiting rather than by reasoning, more by desiring from the depths of our heart than by having a really precise image before our eyes. This is typical of the kingdom of God, its freedom, its spontaneity, its capacity to conquer hearts without forcing them; along with its insignificance and non-visibility.

• *Paul's definitions.* Although Jesus did not waste efforts defining the kingdom and was rather reluctant and sparing in doing so, St Paul in particular offers us some greater clarity in his apostolic letters: they say little about it but what they do say is very convincing and concise.

– I am thinking of Rom 14:17: "For the kingdom of God is not food and drink but righteousness and peace and joy in the Holy Spirit." It is a beautiful, quasi-definition of the kingdom: righteousness, but the righteousness of the kingdom, God's merciful righteousness, followed by peace and joy in the Holy Spirit.

– There is another splendid passage of Paul's which does not give a definition but a description of attitudes: "By contrast, the fruit of the Spirit is love, joy, peace, patience, kindness, generosity, faithfulness, gentleness and self-control" (*Gal* 5:22). This is the fruit of the Spirit. It is the kingdom.

———

- I could also quote 1 *Cor* 4;20, a slightly puzzling but illuminating verse: "But I will come to you soon" Paul writes to those who are criticising him, "... and I will find out not the talk of those arrogant people, but their power. For the kingdom of God depends not on talk but on power" (vv. 19-20), power that is firstly and above all the transformation of human life and also the capacity to work miracles through such transformation.

I wanted to bring together some descriptions and definitions of the kingdom so we can understand that it takes a lifetime to enter into the profound meaning of the petition, "Father, thy kingdom come."

Like yeast and seed

The fact that we keep making this petition shows, on the other hand, that *the kingdom of God is not yet here in its fullness.* In fact it is hidden, is yeast, is a seed, is a tiny little plant, a blade of grass and it requires the eyes of faith to discern it.

Today *the power of Satan is certainly more visible,* but we know that all Jesus' work consists in binding such Satanic power - expressed through sin, pride, the search for success, in arrogance and by oppressing others - so that the kingdom may come. "But no one can enter a strong man's house and plunder his property without first tying up the strong man; then indeed the house can be plundered" (*Mk* 3:27).

Jesus is the one who has tied the strong man up. He did so throughout his life and especially in his passion and death;

when he bound Satan he also bound the power of death and conquered it.

In today's world the "strong man" is still in action and in some ways seems to dominate. Despite his apparently overwhelming power, however, our faith discerns the silent presence of the kingdom already at work, opposed to Satan. As seed and yeast it leavens history.

The coming of the kingdom

How does the kingdom come? Certainly not through the power of our works but through the power of God, of Jesus, through the grace of the Holy Spirit. We desire to ask trustingly that Jesus' humble power may be made manifest until it is completely and finally revealed.

Some exegetes discuss whether "Thy kingdom come" means the eschatological end or a kingdom which comes today, day after day. I think it is more consistent with our reflection as a whole to consider the petition to be referring to the present: "Thy kingdom come"; that is, make manifest, O Lord, your humble, discreet, mysterious, modest, meek, convincing power of your truth.

Obviously we are also looking to its final completion: that the kingdom come in its final manifestation, when death will be conquered and there will be no more tears, nor terror, nor violence, "for the first things have passes away" (*Rev* 21:4).

I would like to make a final observation on the coming of this kingdom.

We have seen that the petition is found in Luke in perhaps its most precise context. Nonetheless we know that Chapter 11 in *Luke* is preceded by statements with which Jesus gradually makes the nature of his Kingdom understood.

The first: "The Son of Man must undergo great suffering, and be rejected by the elders, chief priests and scribes, and be killed, and on the third day be raised" (9:22).

The second: "Suddenly they saw two men, Moses and Elijah, talking to him. They appeared in glory and were speaking of his departure, which he was about to accomplish at Jerusalem" (vv. 30-31).

Then there is a third statement: "While everyone was amazed at all that he was doing" and were expecting the kingdom to show itself with power, and expecting defeat of those who opposed it, "he said to his disciples, 'Let these words sink in to your ears: The Son of Man is going to be betrayed into human hands'" (vv. 43-44).

Jesus brings the kingdom about through his passion.

In hope and peace

What then, are the attitudes with which to express this petition, and what attitudes does it suggest?

It seems to me that while what I have tried to explain is valid, the fundamental attitude is not the attempt to make the kingdom come, almost as if we had to draw it down from on high by violence, but an attitude of *hope* and *peace*.

This is Paul's wish: "May the God of hope fill you with

all joy and peace in believing so that you may abound in hope by the power of the Holy Spirit" (Rom 15:13).

This prayer comes from great hope, absolute trust, a total abandonment to the Lord. While we are saying it we would like to walk in Jesus' footsteps. He teaches us how the kingdom comes, by living a life of poverty, love, forgiveness, gift of self to the extent of death.

It is certainly a very demanding petition which takes in the entire Gospel, and we will never succeed in fully understanding it. Its meaning will be revealed to us over the course of time if we pray humbly, and strive to witness to the attitudes indicated by Jesus as typical of the kingdom, beginning with the beatitudes.

2

MEDITATION
"THY WILL BE DONE ON EARTH
AS IT IS IN HEAVEN"

At the beginning of this meditation let me re-read with you some words from Pope John XXIII's *Spiritual Testament* in which he says: "At the moment for saying farewell, or better still, *arrivederci*, I once more remind everyone of what counts in life: blessed Jesus Christ, His Holy Church, His Gospel; and in the Gospel, above all, the *Pater noster* in the spirit and heart of Jesus and the Gospel."

His words strike one because today is the first Friday of the month, traditionally dedicated to the Heart of Jesus. Over these days we are seeking to enter his heart, his prayer, the prayer he taught us and which certainly corresponds to what was in the depths of his intimate awareness.

In the previous meditation we recalled that in the depths of Jesus' awareness he nursed a desire for the kingdom and became aware of how difficult it is to describe it because he, his life, passion, death, resurrection and ascension are the kingdom and so we should nurture his very sentiments in ourselves.

Therefore we ask you, Lord Jesus, for the grace to be able to achieve the same experience Paul speaks of when he exhorts us to "Let the same mind be in you that was in Christ Jesus" (*Phil* 2:5). We ask for the grace to know you intimately through meditation on the prayer of the Our Father in which you put all your heart. Today is the liturgical commemoration of St Gregory the Great, a saint I have always loved very much. Let us entrust to his intercession our desire to fully understand this prayer.

The invocation we would like to reflect on today, "Thy will be done on earth as it is in heaven," is recorded only by Matthew, not Luke. We ask ourselves whether it was Luke who removed it or Matthew who added it. It seems difficult for Luke to have omitted it if it were part of the original prayer. On the other hand it corresponds fully, and we will see this, to the meaning and spirit of the heart of Christ. So these words, while not strictly necessary because the petition for the kingdom to come already includes everything, are very useful and Matthew wanted them included, to say that the kingdom is actually realised when God's will is fulfilled.

Over these days we have been proposing to seek God's will in our lives. As St Ignatius says in his first *Introductory Observation*, the spiritual exercises are intended as ways of "preparing and disposing the soul to rid itself of all inordinate attachments, and, after their removal, of seeking and finding the will of God in the disposition of our life for the salvation of our soul" (No.1).

As background, let us keep in mind the dramatic verses of *Matthew* 26. They show how Jesus struggles to accept the

kingdom despite desiring so much that it come so that the Father's will be done;

> And going a little farther, he threw himself on the ground and prayed, "My Father, if it is possible, let this cup pass from me; yet not what I want but what you want" (v. 39).

And finally:

> Again, he went away for the second time and prayed, "My Father, if this cannot pass unless I drink it, *your will be done*" (v. 42).

This plea of the Our Father, then, is expressed by Jesus in the darkest moment of his life.

Let us ask Our Lady, who always did what was pleasing to God and dedicated herself to it after the angel's announcement, that we may understand what is this will that we want done "on earth as it is in heaven."

Regarding this, after an introduction, I will develop two reflections: God's will in Jesus and the disciples; God's will in us. I will conclude with some considerations on the words "on earth as it is in heaven."

Introductory Comment

God's will can be understood in two ways: as transcendental and as explicit.

We could describe God's *transcendental* will as his overall plan for the universe, the plan which is salvation for all and is presented in perhaps its most beautiful and concise manner by John;

> For God so loved the world that he gave his only Son, so that everyone who believes in him may not perish but may have eternal life.
>
> Indeed God did not send the Son into the world to condemn the world but in order that the world might be saved through him (3:16-17).

This is God's transcendental will which embraces everything, explains all situations, penetrates all the events of history.

Such a universal will is sung by Paul in the marvellous hymn in the *Letter to the Ephesians*, especially 1:9-10:

> ... he has made known to us the mystery of his will according to his good pleasure that he set forth in Christ, as a plan for the fullness of time, to gather up all things in him, things in heaven and things on earth.

And again in *Col* 1:15-20, Paul explains:

> He is the image of the invisible God, the first born of all creation; for in him all things in heaven and on earth were created, things visible and invisible... all things have been created through him and for him.... For in him all the fullness of God was pleased to dwell, and through him God was pleased to reconcile to himself all things, whether on earth or in heaven, by making peace through the blood of his cross.

Here the transcendental will, by reference to the cross, already becomes somehow explicit, that is, more concrete.

In the *First Letter to Timothy*, the Apostle then invites and urges prayer for everyone because "This is right and is acceptable in the sight of God our Saviour, who desires everyone to be saved and to come to the knowledge of the truth" (2;3-4). It is God's overall plan, his will, his plan of salvation for human beings; it is a comfort for us to know that what God wills is being carried out.

– The will of God that we call *explicit* is instead realised in time; it concerns today, the here and now, and should never be separated from the transcendental will.

In particular it is expressed in the Ten Commandments; this is God's will for our time, especially the great Commandment of righteousness:

Jesus replies to the rich young man:

"Why do you ask me about what is good? There is only one who is good. If you wish to enter into life, keep the Commandments." He said to him, "which ones?" And Jesus said, "You shall not murder; you shall not commit adultery; you shall not steal; you shall not bear false witness; Honour your father and mother; also, you shall love your neighbour as yourself: (*Mt* 19:17-19).

Jesus' response on the commandment of love is also splendid:

... One of them, a lawyer, asked him a question to test him. "Teacher, which commandment in the law is the greatest?" He said to him, "*You shall love the Lord your God with all your heart, and with all your soul, and with all your mind.*" This is the greatest and first commandment. And a second is like it: "*You shall love your neighbour as yourself.*" On these two commandments hang all the law and the prophets (*Mt* 22:35-40).

God's will is made explicit in precepts, commands, actions required in order to be as He wants, to be his children, to truly experience the filial spirit.

We find other expressions of God's concrete will in the New Testament, for example:

"So it is not the will of your Father in heaven that one of these little ones should be lost" (Mt 18:14). Another important passage is in the *Letter to the Romans*:

I appeal to you, therefore, brothers and sisters, by the mercies of God, to present your bodies as a living sacrifice, holy and acceptable to God, which is your spiritual worship. Do not be conformed to this world, but be transformed by the renewing of your minds, so that you may discern what is the will of God – what is good and acceptable and perfect 912:1-2).

We also have a very beautiful example of conformity to the explicit divine will in the *Acts of the Apostles* where it is said of David:

... he made David their king. In his testimony about him he said, "I have found David, son of Jesse, to be a man after my heart, who will carry out all my wishes" (13:22).

God's explicit is what makes us his children when we carry it out, makes us will people "after his own heart."

This way we come to the point which affects us most closely: How do I know the will of God? What is pleasing, good and perfect to him?

We will see about getting there step by step.

God's will in Jesus and in the disciples

– Firstly, the Gospels show *Jesus* fully immersed in the Father's will. When he exclaims: "Thy will be done" he is voicing his most profound daily intention: that the kingdom may be brought about by doing God's will.

Let me quote some passages from John.

Jn 6:38: "I have come down from heaven not to do my own will, but the will of him who sent me"; v.40: "This is indeed the will of my Father, that all who see the Son and believe in him may have eternal life." Again in 8:29: "And the one who sent me is with me; he has not left me alone, for I always do what is pleasing to him." This reminds us of that other very beautiful passage where Jesus, beside the well in Samaria, answers the disciples who are asking him to eat: "My food is to do the will of him who sent me and to complete his work" (4:34).

We can contemplate Jesus immersed, transfigured, identified by God's will.

– Adherence to this will also characterised the *disciples*. Let me recall at least one passage form Matthew and one from Mark.

At the end of the Sermon on the Mount we read: "Not everyone who says to me, 'Lord, Lord,' will enter the kingdom of heaven, but only the one who does the will of my Father in heaven" (*Mt* 7:21). So Jesus is emphasising not to keep saying "Lord, Lord," but to do the Father's will.

Jesus conveys this idea even more tenderly and warmly in *Mark's* text: "And looking at those who sat around him, he said, 'Here are my mother and brothers! Whoever does the will of God is my brother and sister and mother.'" By doing God's will we acquire unique intimacy with Jesus who goes beyond the family and affective ties of this world because it is the will of the One who created us, is all for us. And we become all for him: "My beloved is mine and I am his" according to the wording of the *Song of Songs* (2:16).

God's will in us

What is God's will in me, us, the Church, the world?

– It is certainly conveyed very clearly in the commandments and precepts of the Church and also in the prescription of Canon Law though with varying obligatory force depending on the content.

God's will is also expressed through obligations freely taken on toward God and others. In this regard I recall that having followed up some cases of priestly crisis as the bishop of a large diocese with thousands of priests, I

was negatively affected by the fact that even in the most sincere cases people would ask: but what does God want from me? They completely overlooked obligations taken on regarding the Church, the faithful, society, in other words, a fundamental reality for living according to God's will: respecting agreements, commitments taken on, keeping promises. God's will is also found there. Naturally there can be exceptional circumstances and the Church can sometimes go as far as dispensation. Nevertheless when someone has taken on an obligation toward an actual community especially if this has been done publicly, solemnly, one cannot dispense oneself as if it did not exist and as if the only thing that counted was one's personal existence before God. Instead, one is found officially before a community and must take account of one's obligations, the consequences of one's actions, before that community.

However, beyond these precise indications of God's will there are lots of areas still where the Lord can promptly put some requests to us. This is the area of the immediacy of the Spirit. We have already said at the beginning that the retreat is the power, energy, ministry of the Spirit and a ministry of immediacy insofar as it concerns demands other than those God asks of us in commandments and precepts, demands found in no commandment, or precept or Code of Canon Law, because they are part of God's history with me, his immediate word which is up to me to deal with.

Vocation, for example, is part of this perspective. No one is obliged by Canon Law, by the Church, to take it on. It is God's history with me and my response to his word.

In the context of vocation there are also some choices attached to the immediacy of daily contact with God. These are the object of *daily discernment.* I am thinking of times and manner of prayer and rest; the way we regulate friendships and everything regarding the area of apostolic zeal where our choices or initiatives are not obligatory but need to be checked against God's will and so are food for discernment.

Knowing God's will is important for my peace of mind, for my truth, the authenticity of my life which places its trust in the word of Jesus communicated to me through the Spirit. Just the same, it is not easy. How often do we ask, maybe even a bit anxiously: am I really doing God's will? Are the undertakings I have embarked on, the choices I have made, really pleasing to God? Sometimes the question is an anguished one and sometimes the uncertainty can torment us for a long time.

To the question of how we come to know God's will, one question we priests often have put to us by the people is: Does God really want this of me? Perhaps he wants something more that I have not understood? There is no mathematical response to this. Indeed, I believe the Lord places us in a state of some anxiety so that in seeking his will we can purify ourselves, be freed from our intemperate or simply fragile, fanciful desires and truly seek what God wants for us.

To help us in the difficult task of discernment we can have recourse to some "rules" which I would now like to recall, because they could be useful over these days of retreat and also later in our normal existence.

To explain the first and perhaps most certain one, I would like to make use of the icon of Moses on the mountain:

> Moses said, "Show me your glory, I pray." And he said, "I will make all my goodness pass before you, and will proclaim before you the name, 'The Lord'; and I will be gracious to whom I will be gracious and will show mercy on whom I will show mercy." "But," he said, "you cannot see my face; for no one shall see me and live." And the Lord continued "See, there is a place by me where you shall stand on the rock; and while my glory passes by I will put you in a cleft of the rock, and I will cover you with my hand until I have passed by; then I will take away my hand, and you shall see my back; but my face shall not be seen" (*Ex* 33:18-23).

Moses asks to see God's face – which means clearly knowing his will – but he will not see it. However, once God has passed by he will see him from behind.

We understand from this image that God's will is clear especially when we *persevere* in peace. When we persevere with some decision we have taken, maybe a difficult one, including through trials and dryness, and *we feel deeply at peace within*, it is a sign we are doing God's will. We often only come to this realisation *afterwards*; every choice is a risk. I recall one experience I had in Milan when I suggested the initiative of the so-called Samuel Group to young people, saying that if they wanted to know God's will and put their lives at his disposal on a 360° radius, they could

join me on the journey for a year. I held a monthly meeting with the hundreds of young people who generously accepted the proposal, after which I gave them some homework, let's call it, and explained St Ignatius' Rules for the discernment of spirits.

I was struck by the fact that the most anxious of the questions put to me by those young men and women who were intensely involved in this journey was this: but am I really sure I am discovering God's will? I would choose consecrated life, priestly life if I were a hundred per cent sure God wanted this. And I used reply: if you want to be sure, you will never make a decision. Life is a risk and choices, especially those concerning our lives, are risk-filled. They need to be the object of discernment through prayer, advice, reflection; and yet, we will never have the mathematical certainty that our choice corresponds to God's will. It is a certainty we will achieve only over time and by persevering in peace.

I advise you to read two texts from *Isaiah*, which speak of God's support accompanying us in our weakness, culminating in peace:

For thus said the Lord God, the
Holy One of Israel;
In returning and rest you shall be saved;
in quietness and in trust shall be
your strength (30:15).
Have you not known? Have you
not heard?
The LORD is the everlasting God,

the Creator of the ends of the earth.
He does not faint or grow weary;
his understanding is unsearchable.
He gives power to the faint,
and strengthens the powerless.
Even youths will faint and be weary,
and the young will fall exhausted;
but those who wait for the LORD
shall renew their strength,
they shall mount up with wings
like eagles,
they shall run and not be weary,
they shall walk and not faint (40:28-31).

Perseverance in peace is truly a sign of the Lord's will.

There are other ways for discerning and St Ignatius describes them extensively. I will limit myself to recalling at least the passage which describes the *times for making a good choice*, in general.

– The *first time* is "When God our Lord so moves and attracts the will that a devout soul without hesitation, or the possibility of hesitation, follows what has been manifested to it. St Paul and St Matthew acted thus in following Christ our Lord" (No.175).

This is an almost charismatic form of discernment we could say, but it is not so rare. There are choices which are certain, tranquil, choices we have no doubts about (God is asking me and I will jump to it). Personally I have always said that my choice to go to Jerusalem has no logical reason; it is a charismatic choice. I feel consoled and supported in

this by Paul's words in his speech at Miletus where he says: "And now, as a captive to the Spirit, I am on my way to Jerusalem, not knowing what will happen to me there" (Acts 20:22). Charismatic choice does not imply an evaluation of the pros and cons, nor is it a search for some particular mission, but it is rather the influence of the Spirit. And until today, at least, I have not had the least doubt about my choice, which seems to me to be confirmed.

– The *second time* is "when much light and understanding are derived through experience of desolations and consolations and discernment of diverse spirits" (No. 176). There is clarity though not absolute clarity. This is an application of the Rules of Discernment I have already reminded you of: we lean especially toward what the Spirit urges in us, considering where he has us remain happily and where, by contrast, it arouses resentment in us, aversion, in other words working out the pros and cons of the consolations and desolations.

Thus we gradually discover God's will.

So many vocations are born this way: we feel some disgust, or realise how unsatisfying some worldly activity is for us, some emotional attachment or situation. Then we feel called to do something more, through the work of the Spirit attracting us.

The *third* "is a time of tranquillity. One considers first for what purpose man is born, that is, for the praise of God our Lord and for the salvation of his soul." [God's transcendental will] "With the desire to attain this before his mind, he chooses as a means to this end a kind of life or state within

the bounds of the Church that will be a help in the service of his Lord and for the salvation of his soul. I said it is a *time of tranquillity*, that is, a time when the soul is not agitated by different spirits, and has free and peaceful use of its natural powers" (No. 177).

This is a time for being rational, always inspired by faith and the Gospel, but one where we weigh up arguments for and against. This is what happens in many pastoral decisions: they don't come about simply from a charismatic urge but because, once the pros and cons have been reviewed in the light of the Church's teaching, of psychology and sociology, we choose this or that way of acting.

So the heavenly Jerusalem will come

What remains – and it is not so easy – is to comment on the final part of the petition in the Our Father, "on earth as it is in heaven."

It is time that the heaven-earth correspondence occurs most frequently in *Matthew's* Gospel.

In the meditation on "Our Father who art in heaven" I have already quoted the promise made to Peter: "Whatever you bind on earth will be bound in heaven, and whatever you loose on earth will be loosed in heaven" (16:19), repeated in 18:18: "Whatever you bind on earth will be bound in heaven, and whatever you loose on earth will be loosed in heaven"; and I recalled the words: "Again, truly I tell you, if two of you agree on earth about anything you ask, it will be done for you by my Father in heaven" (v.19).

This correspondence, then, is relatively common for Matthew.

I have reflected much on what the expression "on earth as it is in heaven" could mean as a whole. And it seems to me we should firstly stress the fact that we are not dealing with an argument – even if we dwelt at length on our search to know and carry out what God wants – but an invocation. We are asking God to act that his will be done, be it of the transcendental or explicit kind.

In considering this, it seems to me that "*on earth as it is in heaven*" could be translated as: "your will be done," your justice, truth, peace, *with the promptness, elegance, joy, decision, precision with which it is done in heaven.*

If the kingdom of God is the beginning of the heavenly Jerusalem our desire is that the heavenly Jerusalem will finally come, where there are no more tears or sorrow, where former things have passed away, where justice reigns permanently. May it come in fulfilment of all the details of God's will which it is up to us to do in certainty, peace, joy and ease. Our plea is that earth as a whole will shine with the peace and light proper to God's abode, in the fullness of the heavenly Jerusalem.

Lord, you know what you want from us. Often we do not properly know it and perhaps we waste time forever wandering along mistaken paths. Grant us the light and clarity to understand what you expect of us, and the strength to put it into practice serenely, deftly and zealously, just as we contemplate your will being done in heaven.

IN THE FREEDOM
OF THE SPIRIT
(HOMILY)

A model Pastor

Today we celebrate the liturgical Commemoration of St Gregory the Great: St Gregory the monk, bishop, Pope; St Gregory a man of the Word.

It was his powerful intuition that the scripture grows in us as we read it: *Scriptura crescit cum legente.* Also illuminating and comforting for us is another of the experiences he has left us as a testimony: that more than once, when he had not understood a passage of the Scripture, he then understood it when explaining it to the people.

So he is patron of our biblical preaching, patron of our love for the Scripture, the man of the Word.

He is also a man of balance. I learned to appreciate him many years ago when I was living in Rome as a student, then teacher of Scripture. Inwardly over those years I was experiencing many contradictions and emotions and was helped by reading his *Regula pastoralis*, a masterpiece of balance, constant relating of opposites to find the golden mean, so he is a lesson of an extraordinary life for us.

———

Life is made up of opposites, contrariness, opposition; we should always look for the middle way, the way that resolves contradictions, clashes of principles. The *Regula pastoralis* is all about this peaceful resolution of opposites.

I like to recall that I was also helped by finding significant similarity with Gregory's reflections in a work by the young Romano Guardini, *L'opposizione polare* where he too invites one to reject any extremism and constantly re-establish a balance of opposites which supports growth and joy because it allows us to understand the complexity of life.

The breviary today instead gives us something taken from Gregory's *Homilies on Ezekiel*. It brings him very close to us and treats him sympathetically.

He recognises his inability to reach unity in life because he is pushed and pulled from every side. He had to ensure the monks had what they needed, had to look after the townsfolk and their affairs, repel the Barbarians. He recognised that at times he even found himself caught up in gossip, which began with the desire to encourage someone in order to win their favour, but then he willingly gave into it.

He was a very real human being, then, so humble. He recognised his weaknesses, and seeing how confused and torn he was, he entrusted himself to the one who could save him: "Perhaps the very recognition of my faults will obtain forgiveness for me from the merciful judge."

He is truly an extraordinary example of a pastor, even more so for having lived through very sad social, political and ecclesial circumstances – the invasion by the Barbarians,

the failure of all authority, the increasing injustice and acts of violence, difficult relations with the Church in the East. He teaches us that whatever our situation we can become saints. He did not wait for better times, but lived through the tragic difficulties of his own times by doing the Father's will at every moment. By embracing it he found himself immersed in God's holiness.

Thus he becomes a model for every pastor, every bishop in particular crushed by a thousand requests all urgent, necessary, every one more important than the other. So he needed to try to live in peace with such a build-up of urgent matters. He is also a patron of parish priests assailed by demands, requests, complaints, emotional blackmail, and needing to find the way to unity, humility, truth in all of this.

It is a gift of God, and we ask God for it through the intercession of St Gregory.

The law of love

> Then they said to him, "John's disciples, like the disciples of the Pharisees, frequently fast and pray, but your disciples eat and drink," Jesus said to them, "You cannot make wedding guests fast while the bridegroom is with them, can you? The days will come when the bridegroom will be taken away from them, and then they will fast in those days." He also told them a parable: "No one tears a

piece from a new garment and sews it on an old garment; otherwise the new will be torn and the piece from the new will not match the old. And no one puts new wine into old wineskins; otherwise the new wine will burst the skins and will be spilled, and the skins will be destroyed. But new wine must be put into fresh wineskins. And no one after drinking old wine desires new wine, but says, 'The old is good'" (*Lk* 5:33-39).

Luke's passage begins by mentioning the prayer of John's disciples and the Pharisees' disciples. Regarding the former we find just one reference other than this text, in Lk 11:1: "One of his disciples said to him, 'Lord, teach us to pray, as John taught his disciples.'" Two mentions, then, but significant ones.

Regarding the prayers of the Pharisees and their disciples, we have *Mark's* words for example. "They devour widows' houses and for the sake of appearance say long prayers" (12:40). There is the parallel to that in *Luke* (20:47). Both underscore the ostentation and length of the prayers.

Thus we are led to a comparison with the prayer Jesus taught us. And once again the Our Father appears to us in all its worth, like a small miniature, a small jewel where every word can be extended to fit the grandeur of Christ. It contains such impressive understanding and power in its brevity and simplicity.

Jesus then goes on to teach that what counts is the presence of the bridegroom, not the fast.

It is a new way of thinking where it is no longer the law that matters but personal love for Jesus, Jesus as bridegroom and friend in our midst, Jesus as our all.

I am sure we go through various moments in our life regarding our familiarity with Jesus. There are times when it is easy, sweet, joyful. Then as the *Imitation of Christ* puts it, "*esse cum Jesu dulcis*": it is sweet paradise to be with Jesus.

However, when Jesus is silent, then we feel depressed and would like to have the courage to say, like St Theresa of the Infant Jesus: I am a ball Jesus can play with in his hands or throw aside. I know that whatever the case, he loves me.

"It is the Lord who judges me"

Think of us in this way, as servants of Christ and stewards of God's mysteries. However, it is required of stewards that they be found trustworthy. But with me it is a very small thing that I should be judged by you or by any human court. I do not even judge myself. I am not aware of anything against myself, but I am not thereby acquitted. It is the Lord who judges me. Therefore do not pronounce judgement before the time, before the Lord comes, who will bring to light the things now hidden in darkness and will disclose the purposes of the heart. Then each one will receive commendation from God (*1 Cor* 4:1-5).

We can learn great freedom of spirit from the first reading. We cannot even judge ourselves; only God does that. "I am not aware of anything against myself, but I am not thereby acquitted." I should not be concerned, then, about the people's judgement, either the criticisms or praises they heap on me; I do not judge nor acquit myself because it is only the good Lord who can judge and acquit me.

I recall one of my priests, a great theologian, a man of great spirituality, who died of cancer while still young. He said in his spiritual testament: "I am happy to find myself before a judge who gave his life for me; he will judge me and then I will know how much I am worth. I certainly won't be worth much but I know he will love and forgive me. According to Paul's words: 'I do not pronounce judgement before the time, before the Lord comes, who will disclose the purposes of the heart. Then each one will receive commendation from God.'"

We entrust ourselves to you O Lord, the just judge. We are happy not to be able to judge our life at depth, whether we are truly living the Gospel, whether this Church of ours is as fully evangelical as it should be. You know it, Lord, and you will judge us with love and also be able to purify us, because we are yours and all we want is for you to reign in our hearts.

1

MEDITATION
"GIVE US TODAY
OUR DAILY BREAD"

Right at this hour on Friday, in Jerusalem, they are about to set out on the Way of the Cross through the streets of the Old City, finally reaching the altar of Our lady of Sorrows, close to concluding the journey to Calvary and then the Sepulchre. So let us ask Mary's intercession that we might join in that journey which depicts the suffering of Jesus and all of humanity.

There is still one petition in the Our Father we have not considered, the petition for our daily bread. It is the simplest, one could almost say the least interesting, the more modest of them all but maybe the one that affects us more immediately.

It is curious that we ask for this and not other things. I have often said to myself: Why are we not wanting to obtain faith, hope, charity, but simply ask for our daily bread?

Let us try to understand the meaning of these words, then, confident that the spirit can enlighten us as to the depth and truth of what Jesus has asked for.

———

What bread?

By contrast with the first three invocations where the verbal sense seems to dominate or the verb is the important factor ("*Hallowed* be thy name", "Thy kingdom *come*", "Thy will be *done*"), here it is the noun that does so: "Give us this day our *daily bread.*" Grammatical focus is on the bread.

– What is meant by "bread"?

Certainly bread in the material sense, but its meaning could be extended to include daily needs, everything we need and which is essential for our survival.

Bread for which the Greek text uses the word "*emòn*" and adds "*ton epioùsion*". Just what this "bread *ton epioùsion*" is trying to say, no one really knows.

It is a Greek term whose meaning has never been fully clarified even today. It is found only in this passage of scripture and on an ancient papyrus where it is also unclear what it means – perhaps victuals, daily items. Furthermore old versions, which include lots of meanings, confirm for us that the words are difficult to interpret.

The *Vetus Latina* (old Latin) version translated "daily" as we do today; but we do not know how this choice is justified. St Jerome's *Vulgate* translated it as "super-substantial" meaning the heavenly bread, the Eucharistic bread, the bread of the Father's infinite love, the bread of eternal life.

The Syriac version translated it as ""perpetual", showing that it was not just about today, but is given us today for eternity. Another Syriac version says "necessary".

Also interesting is the Sahidic translation: "to come", the bread to come. It could be the more precise grammatical

translation which best renders the meaning of the Greek verb. In another Coptic translation we find "tomorrow's": bread for tomorrow. This would be saying that whoever works each day already has today's bread and since his is paid of an evening, can buy bread for tomorrow.

However, nobody knows precisely which is the best translation The Italian CEI Version [but also the NRSV and others] has chosen "daily" and we hold to this choice because it has a certain logic to it.

– We note last of all, that while the petition in Matthew's text reads: *ton àrton emòn ton epioùsion dos emìn sémeron,* "Give us this day our daily bread,' it reads differently in Luke's Gospel which expresses the same content with different verb forms: *ton àrton emòn ton epioùsion didou emìn lo kath' eméran,* or, "continue to give us each day our daily bread." Luke seems to have a little more foresight insofar as he asks not just for today's bread but bread given each day.

Who is praying like this?

We can enhance this reflection by asking ourselves who is making the petition, who it can best be ascribed to.

Some exegetes, especially those who interpret the Our Father as the prayer Jesus passes on to his *itinerant disciples,* those who set out on the mission without bag and purse (Cf.*Lk* 10:4), maintaining that it is valid for them in the first instance. They have left everything, have nothing, and confidently ask their Father in heaven each day to give them what they need to survive so they can preach the Gospel

today without worrying about tomorrow. The request presumes extreme poverty and trust.

This is certainly the most radical interpretation.

– Obviously, once included within the Gospels, this petition is then adapted to other situations. So, for example, to the *disciple* in general, not simply the itinerant disciple going around without supplies, but every disciple who has decided to follow Jesus and does not depend on wealth, and who is not pretentious, does not want to become rich, is not looking for great security, and only asks for help on a day by day basis.

– The third situation we can glimpse behind the petition is *the person who knows that he or she is fragile*, weak, in a precarious situation, so confides in the Father. It is a beautiful prayer of trust: your Father knows that you need all these things. Your Father provides for the birds of the air, the lilies of the field, and will also provide for you (Cf. *Mt* 6:25 ff.).

In this sense the request for bread corresponds somewhat to the spirituality which shines through the Book of Proverbs, for example, 30:7-9.

Two things I ask of you;
do not deny them to me before I die.
Remove far from me falsehood and lying;
give me neither poverty nor riches;
feed me with the food that I need,
or I shall be full, and deny you,
and say, "Who is the Lord?",
or I shall be poor, and steal,
and profane the name of my God.

We read something similar in Proverbs 27:1-2 which can also serve well as a comment on the request for bread in the Our Father: "Do not boast about tomorrow, for you do not know what a day may bring." In other words, be content with today, be content with what the Lord gives you today, tomorrow will see to itself. This is the spirituality the unforgettable Pope John XXIII called "a contented poverty," the poverty of someone who does not pretend too much, is satisfied with what he has and asks the Lord to give him what is necessary so he does not need to despair, but also has no need to seek wealth so as not to fall into temptation and peril.

Up till now we have considered three situations which come gradually closer to our own: the first is the precariousness of itinerant disciples who have nothing; the second is that of the disciple who has decided to follow Jesus and does not want to depend on wealth and is unpretentious; the third is in regard to the human being in general, who entrusts himself completely to God, knowing that wealth is not sufficient for defending against sickness, death or misfortune.

Let me stress a fourth situation which probably underlies the request for bread: this is the situation of the *faithful who yearn for the bread that is Jesus, for eternal bread*, the bread of plenitude, and who ask for it today. Here we are reconnecting with what was said about the translation of *epioùsion* as "super-substantial", the bread of eternal life.

It is a situation we can read clearly expressed in Chapter 6 of *John's* Gospel:

Then Jesus said to them, "Very truly, I tell you, it was not Moses who gave you the bread from heaven, but it is my Father who gives you the true bread from heaven. *For the bread of God is that which comes down from heaven and gives life to the world.*" They said to him, "Sir, give us this bread always."

Jesus said to them, "I am the bread of life, whoever comes to me will never be hungry, and whoever believes in me will never be thirsty" (vv. 32-35).

These words are then picked up in the same discourse.

I am the bread of life. Your ancestors ate the manna in the wilderness and they died. This is the bread that comes down from heaven, so that one may eat of it and not die. I am the living bread that came down from heaven. Whoever eats of this bread will live forever; and the bread that I will give for the life of the world is my flesh (vv. 48-51).

If we read the commentaries by the Fathers, we see that they shift from one to another of the different meanings. I think it is permissible for us to do so too, asking for our daily needs, entrusting ourselves to the Father as children and asking for the Eucharistic bread.

The petition, "Give us today our daily bread" has very broad contours and each can give it the meaning the Spirit

suggests. However it is a petition which goes to the essence of things and that essence is Jesus.

Humility, filial trust, solidarity

What attitudes does prayer of this kind suggest as gospel attitudes?

I will pick out five.

– It is certainly a prayer of modest folk, not of the rich. It suggests *being happy with what is needed*, not wanting too much, not wanting to have everything, and being grateful for what is given us.

– The second attitude is one of great *filial trust* in the Father. A beautiful translation of this attitude comes to mind, the famous prayer of Charles de Foucauld:

My Father,

I abandon myself to You,

do with me what you want.

Whatever You do with me I will thank you for it.

I am ready for everything, I accept everything.

So long as Your will be done in me,

in all Your creatures.

I desire nought else, my God.

I place my soul in Your hands,

I give it to You, my God,

with all the love I have in my heart,

because I love You,

and because I need love, need to

make a git of myself

to place myself in Your hands, without limits,
without infinite trust.
Because You are my Father.

It is total trust in the Father, today and tomorrow, in life and in death.

– The third attitude is one of *solidarity*. Let us keep in mind that the petition is in the plural: "Give *us* today *our* daily bread." It stirs up our solidarity, our attention to the poor, to those who have no daily bread, to people who suffer hunger. It seems to me that a movement for justice can come from this prayer, to act in a way that everyone can have at least what is necessary to survive on.

– The fourth attitude we are invited to adopt is the one we find strongly expressed in the Sermon on the Mount. We have already pointed to it but I am bringing you back to it because we often forget about it. So often I say to myself So do I truly believe in the words of the Sermon on the Mount and live them? Have I seriously made them my own?

I refer to Mt 6:25-34:

> Therefore I tell you, do not worry about your life, or what you will eat, or what you will drink, or about your body, what you will wear. Is not life more than food, and the body more than clothing? Look at the birds of the air; they neither sow nor reap nor gather into barns, and yet your heavenly Father feeds them. Are you not of more value than they? And can any of you by worrying add a single hour to your span of life? And why do you worry about clothing?

Consider the lilies of the field, how they grow; they neither toil nor spin, yet I tell you, even Solomon in all his glory was not clothed like one of these. But if God so clothed the grass of the field, which is alive today and tomorrow is thrown into the ovens, will he not much more clothe you – you of little faith? Therefore do not worry, saying 'what will we eat?' or 'What will we drink?' or 'What will we wear?' For it is the Gentiles who strive for all these things; and indeed your heavenly Father knows that you need all these things. But strive first for the kingdom of God and his righteousness and all these things will be given you as well so do not worry about tomorrow, for tomorrow will bring worries of its own.

Words of gold. Yet we do not remember them because we are so busy, anxious, and in need of certain, secure, tangible plans that we leave nothing to Providence. Then when Providence surprises us with unexpected events like a misfortune or sudden illness, we see we have depended too much on ourselves.

We are being urged to check out our ability to entrust ourselves to the Father, overcoming our concerns and fear of tomorrow.

– A final attitude comes from our interpreting "bread" as Eucharistic bread: it is *trust in the Eucharist*, our daily bread, *trust in God's word* which we nurture ourselves with daily. This food has the power to sustain and comfort

us, to confirm us and make us persevere. We will not make it alone but may the Eucharistic bread, the bread of the Word, humbly requested in prayer, save us from temptation and give us the perseverance which can respond to God's promises.

CONCLUSION

It would have been good to have had the time to provide a résumé, a complete overview of the Our Father, reading into its petitions Jesus' passion, glory and resurrection, and the Trinity. In my view this is the concluding point.

The Trinity is there because *we are calling on the Father who is "in heaven"*, where the fire of that Love that spreads throughout the world begins from, that torrent of dedication and Love which is the Trinitarian Mystery: the Father generates the Son in the Holy Spirit.

The Trinity is present because it *operates through Jesus*.

He is the one *par excellence* who *hallows the Father's name*, who is the holy one, the consecrated one sent into the world. It is he who "was declared to be Son of God with power according to the spirit of holiness by resurrection from the dead" (Rom 1:4), the one who also sanctifies himself for us, until in turn we are sanctified in truth.

Jesus *is the kingdom* which comes through his preaching, his miracles, his passion and glory. Through all this he *perfectly accomplishes the Father's will* which is his food. "And it is by God's will that we have been sanctified

---

through the offering of the body of Jesus Christ once for all" (*Heb* 10:10) but present in every *Eucharist*, in the *daily bread* in which the Mystery of the Son, the Father and the Holy Spirit is given us invincibly.

Through the power of the Spirit Jesus *forgives sins* – "Receive the Holy Spirit. If you forgive the sins of any, they are forgiven them" (*Jn* 20:22-23), the Spirit who defends us in temptation: "he will prove the world wrong about sin and righteousness and judgement" (*Jn* 16:8).

And only through the power of the Holy Spirit does Jesus *deliver us from evil*.

I leave it up to you to further explore this summary reading of things. Ignatius writes that whoever offers meditations is only offering some stimulus which retreatants can then work on, including after the retreat has finished, recalling all the richness of God's word.

Let us remain united in this Word, which is a light for our steps, and I entrust it to you so that beyond any resistance of ours, it will have the power to sanctify us and make us live like Jesus.

CARLO MARIA MARTINI
Foundation

The Carlo Maria Martini Foundation came into existence through the initiative of the Italian Province of the Jesuits and with the involvement of the Archdiocese of Milan. It aims at remembering Cardinal Carlo Maria Martini by promoting knowledge and study of his life and works and keeping alive the spirit that animated his commitment, encouraging experience and knowledge of the Word of God in the context of our contemporary culture.

With this in mind, the Foundation's role is spelt out in a number of specific actions:

- Bringing the Cardinal's works, writings and addresses together in an archive and promoting their study as well as encouraging and authorising their publication.
- Supporting and nurturing ecumenical and inter-religious dialogue, with civil society and non-believers as well, working closely together to understand the indissoluble connection between faith, justice and culture.
- Fostering the study of Scripture involving other disciplines, including spirituality and social sciences.
- Contributing to pastoral and formative projects valuing Ignatian pedagogy and addressed especially to the young.
- Supporting study of the meaning and extended practice of the Spiritual Exercises.

Those who wish to can contribute to the collection of materials (written, audio, video) on Cardinal Martini by indicating initiatives regarding him by writing to segretaria@fondazionecarlomariamartini.it

To subscribe to the newsletter (in Italian) and support the Foundation's activities: www.fondazionecarlomariamartini.it

BIBLICAL MEDITATIONS

A selection of sermons, retreats and meditation texts drawn from the vast work of Cardinal Martini. There is a roundup of biblical personalities from Old and New Testaments, explanations, some chosen topics to accompany reflections on the human being in search of God. The inestimable legacy of a man of prayer and contemporary spirituality.

1. **The Accounts of the Passion.** Meditations
2. **Paul.** In the midst of the ministry
3. **Our Father.** Do not heap up empty phrases
4. **The Apostles.** Men of peace and reconciliation
5. **Abraham.** Our father in faith
6. **Jesus.** Why He spoke in parables?
7. **Elijah.** The living God
8. **Stephen.** Servant and witness
9. **Peter.** Confessions
10. **Jacob.** A man's dream
11. **Jeremiah.** A prophetic voice in the city
12. **Israel.** A people on the move.
13. **Samuel.** Religious and civil prophet
14. **Timothy.** Timothy's way

CPSIA information can be obtained
at www.ICGtesting.com
Printed in the USA
BVHW030335090620
581139BV00002BA/6/J